TACOS ON THE TUNDRA

TACOS ON THE TUNDRA

The story of Barrow, Alaska's long-time resident, Fran Tate

by
Lyn Kidder
Photographs by Frederic Moras

BONAPARTE BOOKS

Copyright © 1996 by Lyn Kidder
All Rights Reserved
First Edition
First Printing 1996
ISBN 0-9654826-2-6
Library of Congress   1. Barrow (Alaska)—Description and travel.
                      2. Business—Alaska—Biography.
                      3. Tate, Fran (1929 –   )
Published in the United States of America by Bonaparte Books.
Editing: Kathy MacKenzie, Powell, Wyoming.
Design and Layout: The Big Empty Imaging Co., Powell, Wyoming.
Film Output: Northland Graphics, Flagstaff, Arizona.
Printing: Aspen Printing, Flagstaff, Arizona.
        Printed on recycled paper.

No part of this book may be reproduced, published or transmitted in any form or by any means, electronic or mechanical, including photocopying, recording or by any information storage and retrieval system without express permission of the publisher.

To my husband Frederic, who came home from work one day and said, "You know, someone ought to write a book about Fran…"

Tacos on the Tundra
contents

Taco Tuesday *1*
Beginnings *11*
School....................................... *21*
Love and Marriages........................... *30*
The Original Pepe............................ *49*
The Age of Aquarius *54*
The Spy Who Came into the Cold *59*
Life at the Top of the World.................. *71*
Pepe's—Opening Soon.......................... *85*
The Restaurant Biz *98*
Pepe's II *108*
Joe the Waterman............................. *115*
Troubles *130*
Heeere's Franny!............................. *141*
Saving the Whales *150*
Diabetes *168*
Steve and Johnnie *183*
Community................................... *190*
Jazz Below Zero *200*
Boss Lady *208*
Tourists..................................... *219*
The One-Woman Chamber of Commerce............ *225*
The Polar Bear Club *228*
The Japanese Connection...................... *235*
The Christmas Card Queen..................... *245*
Work *253*
The World According to Fran.................. *261*

Chapter 1
Taco Tuesday

It's a typical lunch hour rush at Pepe's North of the Border, the world's northernmost Mexican restaurant. It's Taco Tuesday, a few days after the last sunrise of the year. The lure of $1 off the price of tacos brings a substantial part of Barrow's working population in from the nearby courthouse, bank, and office buildings of the Arctic Slope Regional Corporation and the North Slope Borough. A pink crescent moon hangs low over the frozen ocean. The sky is a rich midnight blue and although the horizon beyond the airport is rosy, most of the cars cruising the snow-packed streets have their headlights on. The parking lot next to Pepe's fills up with pick-ups, vans and other utilitarian vehicles, many of them carrying official insignia of the North Slope Borough, the City of Barrow, or the State of Alaska. It's been minus 20 and colder for weeks, and since the building has no outlets for plugging in the vehicles, many of them are left running. Car theft is not a concern; with only 45 miles of road around Barrow—and none of them going anywhere—there's not much incentive.

The building that houses Pepe's is a one-story, nearly windowless mustard-colored rectangle perched 7 feet above the ground on pilings—typical modern arctic architecture. Most large, heated buildings in the Arctic are constructed this way, since putting them directly on the ground would melt the permafrost, settling them into a swamp of their own making. Pepe's mascot, a bow-legged guy in a parka and sombrero, decorates two sides of the building. A double stairway made of open metal grating (another feature of arctic architecture) leads to the front door. Red and yellow Christmas lights shine along the roof edge.

The battered front doors open into an arctic entryway (known to most Barrow residents by the Iñupiaq name *qanitchaq* and pronounced "kunnychuck"), a sort of vestibule that reduces the impact of icy winds. Past the qanitchaq, the interior of the restaurant is divided into three sections. The Coffee Shop, just inside the entrance, is outfitted with standard booths and decorated with piñatas, with long gray pieces of bowhead whale baleen, and—for the holidays—masses of poinsettias. A hallway leads to dining rooms on either side of the building, the Fiesta Room to the right and El Toro to the left.

Appropriately enough, bulls' horns hang over the doors in El Toro. Murals, painted by a Barrow local of Peruvian origin, continue the matador theme on the largest wall. A raised platform runs along one side of the room, and little walls with arched Spanish-style windows separate the tables on it from each other. Painted tiles decorate the walls and tables. An oval counter surrounds a raised fireplace capped by a black metal hood. It's a gas fireplace, to be sure (the nearest tree is at least 500 miles away), but it gives diners the warm, cozy feeling that fireplaces inspire. The ceiling is hidden by a line of vividly colored rectangular cloth banners, and the walls are hung with serapes, sombreros, and a *china poblada* skirt and blouse glistening with sequins, made for Fran by a mariachi's mother.

Fran pops out of the swinging doors that lead to the kitchen. She is dressed in a bright red sweater and a pair of white jeans. A red bow at the top of her head pulls back waist-length, pale blond hair. Small and lithe, one would possibly guess her age to be 40. She'll never see 60 again.

El Toro is filling up, many of the customers, Native and non-Native, wearing knee-length parkas with hoods circled with fur. Wolf is the fur of choice because one's breath supposedly will not freeze on it. Fran greets nearly everyone by name, asking about regulars who are not there and catching up on the news.

New placemats are on the tables, showing "Feliz Navidad" and a wreath made from chili peppers. As Christmas nears, the rooms will be crammed with lights and decorations. Fran likes to observe the passing holidays and seasons. One April 15, she made placemats from photocopied 1040 forms, and the menu featured Hobo

Tacos on the Tundra

Stew and biscuits for $10.40. One customer came in, stared at the placemat for a moment, crumpled it up and threw it across the room.

Each table holds a one-page "newspaper" that Fran puts together each morning, made up of local weather, cartoons, news clips from local radio station KBRW's Associated Press wire service, and whatever else she thinks is interesting. In a town where the morning paper arrives on the first plane and usually is unavailable until after noon, people enjoy reading Fran's news. Today's issue has an item on why women feel the cold more than men (more body fat), a thought for the day ("Superstition is the religion of feeble minds"—Edmund Burke), and the fact that today jazz trumpeter Chuck Mangione and Bob Green, the manager of Pepe's, are celebrating birthdays.

At the top of the page is a cartoon of a skinny woman wearing huge galoshes. She's running, her long hair streaming out behind her. One hand holds a loaded tray overhead, the other holds a water hose. An overturned bucket lies behind her. The drawing is a symbol for Tate Enterprises, and it is a cartoon summary of the varied and fast-paced life Fran has led in Barrow for more than two decades.

Every table in El Toro is full and the room is noisy. Bursts of laughter mix with crackles from the two-way radios that many of the customers carry as part of their jobs. Fran moves among the tables, reminding everyone that since it's Bob's birthday, the drinks (non-alcoholic ones in this currently dry town) are on the house. She takes an order from a table of a dozen, nodding as each one in turn recites his or her request. She never writes anything down; a table of twelve is small potatoes for her memory. People have bet money that she couldn't remember orders from a table of 20 or 30. People have bet, and they've lost.

Margaret Grey, an Iñupiat elder known to nearly everyone by her nickname "Magee," peers out of the large front window of her small green house. Her father built the house from the remains of a shipwreck and it stands just across the street from Pepe's. Magee has a standing order for her Tuesday taco, which is personally delivered each week by one of the waiters.

Back in the kitchen, the crew is ready to send out trays for a catered luncheon meeting and a few sheet cakes for other functions. Nothing too elaborate—nothing like the recent 4-day school district in-service to which Pepe's dispatched food for 500 people three or four times a day. Nothing like the upcoming Hawaiian luau theme Christmas party, complete with two whole roast pigs. Just some sandwiches and a few cakes.

Pepe's caters just about everything that happens in a town that can't have a meeting without food. For big events, Fran writes a daily schedule for each employee. During the school district in-service, the final day's schedule for one poor fellow read: "Grand Finale! Only 450 box lunches to fix." It went on to detail exactly how many pickles and cartons of coleslaw and club sandwiches were needed by noon.

Taxi cab drivers arrive to pick up carry-out orders for those who are not venturing out for lunch. Pepe's doesn't deliver, but they'll call a cab, and Barrow's three cab companies send about 30 vehicles out into the streets every day. The cab driver picks up three cheeseburgers and a nacho plate, pays the $25.75 and takes off. He'll add the $4 cab fare when he collects from the customer.

Pepe's is not and never was the only restaurant in Barrow. But it was the first place in town where, as one customer put it, "you could sit down and have a nice dinner in a beautiful atmosphere, and think that you were someplace other than Barrow—if you happened to need to think you were someplace other than Barrow." A woman who met her future husband in Barrow said, "If we were going out on a date, Pepe's was the place to go."

Three hundred miles above the Arctic Circle, Barrow is the northern-most city in the United States. It clings to the last bit of a vast coastal plain that slopes down from the Brooks Range some 200 miles to the south. It lies about equidistant between the state capital of Juneau and the North Pole.

From the air, Barrow looks vulnerable and impossibly small. In summer, the tundra extends in endless miles of brown and green, the ground broken into polygonal shapes outlined by silvery flashes of reflected water. The water comes from a brief annual melting of the surface permafrost. Two feet below the surface the soil is frozen hard, and has been since the age of the woolly mammoths. In late fall, the ocean freezes and the first snows make land and sea nearly indistinguishable. Barrow then looks like a small smudge on a vast paper plate. Its airport is one of those in which passengers leave a jet aircraft and walk through snow, ice, slush, or mud to the terminal. There are tales of new arrivals who took their first close look at the smudge and got right back on the plane.

At the moment, the population of Barrow is about 4,000. About 60 percent of the people are Iñupiat, and their occupation of this site dates back at least 4,000 years. About a tenth of the population is, incongruously, Filipino. The rest of the *tanik,* or non-Native, population—as well as the 8,000 tourists who venture to the North Slope each year—is made up of a broad representation of Europe, Asia, the Caribbean, and the lower 48 states.

Barrow is famous for the "Midnight Sun" and its less-mentioned corollary, the "Midday Darkness." In summer the sun traces a huge circle around the sky, never setting between May 10 and August 2. On August 15, it's possible to enjoy two sunsets in one day, one just after and another just before two midnights. In winter, the sun drops below the horizon on November 18 and does not appear again until January 22.

Right now, it's a long time until sunrise, and the lunch hour is nearly over. Customers shrug into their heavy

Tacos on the Tundra

parkas and repocket their radios. Fran slides around the room, clearing tables as she continues to visit with the customers.

"I've finally got the locals trained," she said. "The whole town takes lunch between twelve and one o'clock. They'd all pour in here, and if they had to wait five minutes, they'd say, 'I've got to be back to work at one.' Well, what else is new? So do the other seventy-five people who are in here! They don't say that no more."

Fran's son, Joe the Waterman, breezes in, grabs some milk from the kitchen and starts out again.

"Ripping off the milk again?" Fran asks.

"Don't I get a discount? How about a senior discount? I better take it now, I'll never live long enough to get it, you'll run me into the ground." The two smile warmly at each other and Joe takes off.

A young black boy, perhaps 10 years old, comes into the restaurant with a gift box. It's a large brass medallion, a present for Fran from Korea. Jamari Floyd just returned from six weeks of taekwondo training in Korea, a trip that Fran helped sponsor with a check.

"There's some kids here in Barrow who could go on to the year 2000 Olympics in Australia," Fran said. "I'm keeping my eye on them."

The boy gives her a hug and leaves. Fran turns to take a phone call behind the cash register, surrounded by an assortment of Pepe's T-shirts, sweatshirts, baseball jackets and hats. One shirt has a neon pink whale and the legend

"Maktak capital of the world." (*Maktak* is the skin and several inches of fat from the bowhead whale—an Iñupiaq delicacy.) Another shirt says, "If our food and service don't meet your standards, lower your standards!" There is a close-out sale on a black T-shirt for the Elephant Pot Sewage Hauling company that carries the motto: "We clean up your act because we've got our shit together."

Fran ends the conversation by slamming down the phone and shouting for her all-around handyman and expeditor.

"Matt! They sent me a thousand pounds of ground beef instead of a hundred, and forty-five pounds of blue cheese instead of fifteen! You load it up and take it all out to the airport and send it back—freight collect! Stupid so-and-so's—they don't know their back end from a can of film!"

CHAPTER 2
Beginnings

A sepia-tone portrait in an oval frame hangs near the entrance to the Fiesta Room. It shows a serious-looking couple, the woman with her dark hair gathered sedately back, the man with a jaunty moustache. Next to it hang framed certificates stating that the names of Theresa Maria Bingesar, of Germany, and Frank Joseph Pfulg, of Switzerland, are inscribed on the 1,000-foot long American Immigrant Wall of Honor at Ellis Island. The couple, along with 17 million other immigrants, entered the United States by way of that famous gateway to the New World.

In the early 1920s, Theresa Maria was living in Switzerland, working as a housekeeper and cook, and "keeping company" with Frank Joseph Pfulg. An athletic young Swiss five years her junior, he was a bicycle racer and champion ski jumper. Frank, who worked on his mother's goat farm, wanted to get married, but Theresa, for some reason, was unwilling.

To escape the situation, she came to America, leaving nine brothers and sisters in Germany and her would-be suitor on his mother's goat farm. She passed through Ellis Island and settled in Washington State, where a Swiss family hired her as a housekeeper. She arrived in America on April 7, 1925. She was 30 years old.

Undiscouraged by this intercontinental romance, Frank kept writing. His letters must have been persuasive, for on December 7, 1925, using funds supplied by his future bride, he too arrived in America. Perhaps believing in the luck of sevens, the couple were married the following year on the anniversary of Theresa's arrival in America—April 7, 1926.

Frank's namesake and only child Fran would later describe her father: "He was just a poor Alps boy. His mom was six foot three, weighed three hundred pounds and had a big goat farm up in the mountains. My father and his sister Johanna were products of their mother and the goat milker. Those things went on, even back in those days. My dad just did farm work and blacksmithing work, he never had any money. So my mom sent him money."

Frank began his new life in America as a dairy hand, working for larger Swiss farmers in Washington State and earning $1.25 a day. Even with this modest income, the couple had a chance to buy a small house near the town of Auburn. It was in that house that Frances Mary Pfulg was born on October 5, 1929.

BEGINNINGS

Unfortunately, the new immigrants didn't understand the financial mechanics of a second mortgage, and the woman who was the real owner of the house arrived in the middle of the night and evicted the young family. It seems fitting that Fran, who would live most of her life at the end of the proverbial shoestring, spent her earliest years living in a berry patch.

"My dad pitched a tent in a berry patch that belonged to friends who lived up the hill," she said. "We lived in the tent in that berry patch from the time I was one or two until I was four years old. I remember the tent, and how much fun it was to run up and down the rows of the berry patch, playing." Her father continued to work as a dairy hand and cut and sold wood. Her mother planted a vegetable garden near their tent. After living several years in the tent, her father rented 125 acres of land and began raising goats and chickens.

"They rented the place for $25 a month, but sometimes even that was hard for them to pay. Sometimes they'd pay with eggs," Fran said. Her father built a small, two-room house—a "tar paper shack," Fran called it.

"There was just the bedroom and the 'other room.' There was a woodstove, and a big oak table with about five legs that somebody gave them. We had to carry our water, so there were a couple five-gallon buckets and a dipper. Next to the wood stove there was a woodbox that I had to keep filled. There was a big wooden hutch where we kept dishes and groceries. My parents bought a little piano, but it was still big enough that it stuck out into the doorway between the two rooms. I remember the Christmas tree went up on the piano. We had those little holders that clipped on the tree and a candle went in them, and that was our Christmas lights.

"We didn't have electricity for the first couple years. When I graduated from high school, we still didn't have running water. I had to carry water from the well, and it was uphill. My dad gave me those two five-gallon buckets and I filled them up, but by the time I got back to the house, my socks and shoes were full of water, and I had only about half a bucket of water. I finally decided I'd make extra trips and only carry half a bucket at a time."

Her father went to work for Freuhauser, a Seattle company that manufactured truck bodies, but continued to farm until his retirement. He built three chicken houses and the family cared for 3,000 chickens and 150 goats. Even as a child, Fran was expected to do her share.

"From the time I was five," she said, "every morning before school I'd help my daddy feed and milk the goats." She helped her father cut wood, holding one end of the big drag saw to keep it from vibrating, and stacking the cut pieces in their truck.

"My daddy didn't want any kids, but if anything he wanted a boy. I was a girl but I kind of became a boy. I think he had a bad experience, since his mother never got married, and my daddy and his sister kept their mother's name. His sister got married but never had any kids either."

Her father, himself athletic, applauded his daughter's physical abilities.

"I'd do somersaults across the floor all through the house, and my mom would yell, 'Stop that, you're going to break your neck!' But my dad would clap and say, 'Looks good.' He hung a rope in a tree and I'd shimmy up, grab the rope and then swing down. My mom would have a fit.

"Our family's name was so stupid. Even for the Swiss. Nobody can say it. It's spelled 'Pfulg.' People pronounced it 'Plug' or 'Fluge.'

"During the Depression, salesmen would come around all the time, and my mother would sometimes order things from them. Then they'd say, 'How do you spell that?' And she'd say, 'P-F-U-L-G.'

"One day when I was about two, we were out in the strawberry patch and a salesman came to sign her up for the newspaper. And when he asked, 'How so you spell that?' I piped right up and said, 'P-F-U-L-G.' I must have heard that so many times, I was brain-washed. 'P-F-U-L-G.' My mom and dad couldn't believe it, they were so proud they rushed in and got the camera. I've got a picture that they took of me right after that, in some skimpy little outfit, with my belly button sticking out.

"One time they were planting potatoes, and of course they had me with them all the time. My dad dug the hole, then my mom would put half a potato in the hole and cover it up with a little hand shovel. They had a big bathtub full of half potatoes, and she had me bring them to her. I was about two or three years old. I'd go over to the bath tub and bring over a potato and drop it in the hole and then go back for another one. She said after about six trips I started loading as many as I could in my little arms so I wouldn't have to make so many trips. So I learned to work very early. That kind of training you get never hurts. I was working smart already.

"German people and the Swiss are very hard workers. I didn't know any word like 'vacation.' In fact, that got me in trouble with my first and last lie.

"When you came to school the first day, the teacher would say, 'Tell us about your vacation.' I remember one girl said, 'We went to Carmel.' I didn't even know where Carmel was. Then the next one went to New York City, and the next one to Atlanta, Georgia. I thought, 'I don't know where half those places are.'

"And I don't have any relatives in this country. I was an only child. And everyone said they went to visit their grandmother, or their Aunt Mattie. I thought, 'I ain't got nobody.'

"But by the time she got to the Ps, where I was, I already had a story cooked up. I can't remember where I said I went, but I said I went with 'Aunt Helen.' I remembered my mother talking about her sister Helen, and how much she hated her because she was the only blonde in the family, and everyone favored her. Anyway, the teacher asked, 'What did you do?' Well, I didn't even know what I was talking about. Finally she asked, 'Did you really go?' and I got caught. I had to go stand in front of the class. Boy, I never did that again.

"But one time my family went to Mt. Rainier, which was eighty miles from our house. Neither of them were vacationers, but my dad loved to drive. So we went in his old '35 Chrysler, with him smoking a White Owl cigar. I couldn't hardly see him, it was so smoky. But we drove eighty miles, had a picnic lunch, and drove back. I threw up all the way there and threw up all the way back, because I wasn't used to riding that far in a car. And going up Mt. Rainier, I thought, 'Oh God, we're going over the edge!' You go up and around and then down. The next time they said, 'We're going to take a one-day vacation, do you want to go?' I said, 'No Mommy, I'll just stay home.'"

The woman who would make her mark as a restaurant owner came from a modest culinary tradition.

"We had corn meal mush in the morning, and we'd put milk on it. What was left over my mother would make into little square patties and fry for lunch. In the evening, she'd take the same leftover cornmeal mush and make grits, and she'd make gravy to pour on top. I thought it was great, I didn't know no different. I still love it. I eat it here in the restaurant and everyone says, 'How can you eat that stuff?'"

Her mother also believed that sandwiches of butter, homemade rye bread, and sliced onions would keep her daughter from catching cold.

"It also keeps you from having friends. Everybody at school would say, 'Ugh! Onions!' But I was healthy. I had eleven perfect attendance years in school, out of twelve."

"My mother would make me wear those knit drop-drawer long underwear until I was in the sixth grade, and it was really embarrassing. They hung down below my dress, and in those days you didn't wear jeans to school. So I'd take panties to school and change, then change back into the long underwear to go home.

"The place where we lived is now called Knickerbocker Heights, and they've got $300,000 homes up where the goats used to roam. Our shack would have been right where the road is now."

When Fran was in junior high school, the family took in two children of another Swiss immigrant family. The mother had deserted them and the father was ill, so the Pfulg's brought the boy and girl to live with them in their tiny house. A photo shows Fran and Elizabeth dressed in identical outfits, and the girls, only a year apart, referred to themselves as twins. But the arrangement was not totally agreeable.

"She worked as an usher in a movie theater, but she would never work in a bowling alley or have a paper route like I did," Fran said. "She was at home more, and then my mom would say, 'She takes care of me,' and then I was no good because I was always out working. Later when I came up to Barrow, Elizabeth was married to a guy who never worked. They got my mom to sign a paper so they could have access to her savings. They said it was to help her get groceries, but they were on welfare and at the same time bought a new Chrysler. My mom later realized what they'd done and was mad about it, but it was too late."

Fran's mother didn't become a citizen until she was 72 years old.

"Then she just did it because she was mad. She would always complain about the government, and I'd say, 'What are you complaining about? You can't even vote,' and it finally got her so mad that she became a citizen."

Fran's easy-going father died at the age of 76, but the stubborn Theresa lived to be 95.

Chapter 3
School

Lorraine and Larry Rupert ate a late breakfast in the coffee shop at Pepe's North of the Border. Some 40 years had passed since they last saw Fran. While planning a vacation to Alaska from their home in Portland, Oregon, they decided to venture to what seemed like the end of the world to visit a former fellow student. At Auburn High School in the 1940s, Fran was in the class ahead of them.

"She was quiet, she wasn't a socialite," Lorraine remembered. "She was hard-working and very bright. Even in the beginning, she cut her way through what was a male-dominated world. The way people thought about her was, if you wanted a job done and done well, you asked Fran."

Fran's school record shows high marks for dependability, initiative and accuracy, but only average marks for personal appearance and sociability. Her yearbook carries the legend "By the work one knows the workman" next to her name and lists her activities: string ensemble, school play, yearbook staff, newspaper editor, Junior Red Cross, Honor Society, Spanish and Latin Clubs, and the student council. In ninth grade she received the American Legion award for "outstanding citizenship and scholastic attainment."

"We worked on the school newspaper together, *The Trojan Trumpet*, when she was the editor in her senior year," Lorraine continued. "I liked her. She was always friendly. We weren't close, but I don't think she was really that close to any of the girls. She was kind of a loner.

"I also remember they wouldn't let her take mechanical drawing, because that was for boys. Girls were supposed to take home ec."

Fran remembered home ec. "I had mostly A's, but I graduated with a 3.76 because of that silly-ass home ec. I can't sew and I can't cook. But in the eighth grade we had to take home ec. The teacher's name was Helen Alexander. I remember her hairdo—what a nerd. It was tight and curly with a little thatch sticking out. And she was never married, so she never cooked for anybody.

"I had such a hard time in that class. It didn't matter if the white sauce was supposed to be thick or thin, I just ruined it. It was either runny as water or I burned it up in the pan.

"Then we were supposed to make a dress. It was World War II, and you couldn't buy material, so we were told to bring one of our mother's old dresses to school and redo it.

"Well, my mother was different from the other mothers.

School

She was thirty-five years older than I was, and a bull-headed German. She bought her clothes at the Goodwill or the Salvation Army. I didn't know about it then, but the dresses she had were made on the bias, so you could take that dress and pull it in any direction you wanted. When you tried to cut a straight line, it looked like you cut it with pinking shears, and the line was never straight.

"My mom had a sewing machine that you worked with a treadle. But at school we had electric machines with a lever that stuck out, and you pushed the lever with your knee. You'd hear it hum and then suddenly it would take off. So I'd get everything all lined up, and try to keep my fingers out from under the needle, and then the machine would just take off and the whole thing would be shot. I'd have to take the scissors out and cut some more off and start all over again. By the end of the quarter, I still wasn't finished, so I had to take it home and finish it over the summer. Well, that was great—I just got my mom to finish it.

"Then to graduate, I had to have one more year of home ec. I waited until my senior year, put it off as long as possible. And here that old battle ax got transferred to the senior high school during my senior year. And she wasn't any happier about it than I was.

"Same thing. Cooking. I didn't cook at home. I didn't want to be a cook. I had no thoughts of being married. My mom was a lousy cook, but I didn't know it then. She'd burn everything because she was always in a hurry. She'd

23

come in from the farm work after taking care of a couple thousand chickens, and she'd cook something quick and throw it on the table. My dad was an old Swiss country boy, he didn't care, he'd eat anything, whatever she threw.

"And every night after my paper route, from the time I was eleven years old until I graduated from high school, I ate dinner at the same restaurant. It was Jack's Cafe, a long, narrow place with about fifteen stools at the counter and three or four booths on one side. I'd just open the door and this woman named Clara would get me a tuna fish sandwich on whole wheat bread and a glass of milk. I'd just sit down, eat it, pay 75 cents and go to my job at the bowling alley. That was my dinner every day. To me, tuna fish was a treat, because my mom never bought tuna fish.

"I got to home ec in the twelfth grade, and the war was over so we bought material and we were going to make a dress. By the time I got through with it, the dress wasn't wide enough, I couldn't get into it. I couldn't get my arm in the sleeve hole.

"That teacher embarrassed me continually. She'd hold up the dress in front of the class and say, 'And this is the work of Frances Pfulg.' It was just terrible.

"I had A's in physics, A's in chemistry. The boys in my class who wanted to be engineers—they didn't have to take home ec. They'd have flunked it, too. It's nice to learn the basics for living, but there are people out there who open restaurants and make clothing. That's why they have companies like that, so you don't have to do that stuff for yourself.

"My senior year I got the same bad mark that I got in the eighth grade, and it made me mad. It still makes me mad. When I got Pepe's and the Burger Barn, I'd say, 'If Miss Alexander knew that I owned two restaurants, she'd roll over in her grave.'"

While attending high school, Fran decided to be an interpreter, learning Japanese from her neighbors, German at home, and studying Spanish and Latin. She was perhaps inspired by her father's sister, who worked as an interpreter in Switzerland. Growing up with immigrant parents, she picked up languages easily in her childhood, although she claims, "I'm never sure when I'm speaking German if the words are German or 'Schweizer Deutch.'"

"I was a loner," Fran remembered. "First of all, I had good grades. Then, I wasn't good-looking, and I dressed old-fashioned. My mom was older than other moms, and she dressed me so I wouldn't catch a cold, in long underwear, high boots and ugly dresses. So I wasn't popular. I never went to any football games because I was always working.

"But they had this dance, called a 'to-lo,' the reverse of the prom because the girl asked the guy out, and then she paid the way. I thought this would give me a chance to take somebody to a dance, and I'd take that night off from working at the bowling alley.

"There was a guy in my class who always had straight A's with no effort. I don't think he ever took a book home. He was just smart. His mother was the city librarian and his dad owned the local newspaper. He finally got a scholarship to Stanford, was a major in World War II in the Marine Air Force, and the last I heard he was working in the Pentagon. But in the tenth grade he was just another student. And I liked him. He was in my chemistry class, physics class, geometry class, calculus class. So I called him to ask him to go to this to-lo.

"His mother answered the phone. She said he wasn't around, and asked what I wanted. I was stupid in asking her, but I'd never done this so I didn't know any better. I said, 'I just wanted to know if Jack would go to the to-lo with me a week from Friday.' And she said, 'Definitely not. Jack wouldn't go with a girl like you. So don't bother to call again.'

"So I cried, and I didn't know what to do. But he wanted to be an engineer. So the next day when I went to school, I went to my guidance counselor and said that I'd changed my mind, that I didn't want to be an interpreter, I wanted to be an engineer. I took a different way, just to challenge him.

"I made it, but I never went as far as he did in the field. But he's the guy that changed my life, just over that phone call. It's incredible how people can be so cruel. But that's what turned me from being an interpreter to being an engineer. Just over some guy."

Fran poured more coffee for Larry and Lorraine. Larry remembered a paper route that he had for the *Seattle*

SCHOOL

Times. They discovered that Fran had taken over the same route when he quit. "But I didn't go past Western Avenue," Larry recalled.

"I went way out there in the country," Fran said, "about five miles on my bicycle, and sometimes it would be raining, thunder and lightning, and I'd be out there just pedaling away." She still has a letter, dated June 28, 1945, from the country circulation manager of the *Times.* A florid engraved letterhead covers the top quarter of the page, and the yellowing envelope is stamped with a 3-cent stamp. The letter says, "Many, many thanks for the splendid work you have done for us."

Fran took on the paper route when she was 11 years old, and continued to deliver the *Times* until she graduated from high school. She began the habit of filling every waking hour with work, a habit that she would later continue in Barrow. When she was 12, she got her job at the bowling alley, setting pins.

"I started the paper route at three-thirty, after school, got to the bowling alley at seven, worked until midnight and then rode my bicycle home."

Lorraine said, "I was never supposed to be around the bowling alleys. They had a bad reputation."

"I wasn't really my daddy's friend for quite some time," Fran said. After I started working in the bowling alley, then he was proud of me. My mom didn't like me working in the bowling alley. At first we set the pins by hand. Later they got a rack that you filled and then dropped down, but

27

you could still get hit. It was hard work. I was just a little wimp, but I was strong from working on the chicken farm.

"It was just the riff-raff working back there, really foul-mouthed guys, guys that couldn't even get a job washing dishes. My mother couldn't believe that my dad wanted me to work in the bowling alley, but he was a good bowler. I knew if I was going to be a tomboy and be my dad's friend, that's what I had to do.

"My mom went to the principal and said that if my grades lowered by one point, I'd have to quit the job. My dad said, 'No, my little Schatzalie—my little sweetheart—she's gonna to do all right.' And I did. My grades never dropped, and I kept that job until the night before I graduated from high school.

"But those sleazy guys never bothered me. They were ten years older than me, but they never bothered me. I got hurt a lot of times, setting the pins. When the ball came, you had to put your legs up, get out of the way. Sometimes the pins would fly up. My dad threw a wicked ball, they'd fly up and hit you on the back of the leg. You'd have to watch you didn't get hit in the head. I'd put my arm up and then get hit in the arm. And if it hit your elbow, you'd about die.

"There was one guy who wasn't a fighter, but he bit cops all the time when they tried to arrest him. Even he wouldn't set pins for my dad, so I always had to do it. Seven cents a line we got, for each game, for each person. When the leagues played, there were five men on a league and they play three games each, so that's fifteen games times seven cents. That's what I got."

Fran went off to answer the phone. Lowering her voice, Lorraine said, "Her family didn't help her at all—they didn't know how. Everything she's done, she's done on her own."

Larry added, "Unlike the rest of us, Fran never really left Auburn. She went to the University of Washington, and then came back to Auburn and stayed there. Right up until she came up to Barrow. When she finally made a change, it was a big one."

Fran stopped by the table. "If you're talking about me, don't tell them I'm a floozy."

Then she added, "This is better than going to a high school reunion. This way I don't have to see the ones I don't want to see."

Chapter 4
Love and Marriages

If she hasn't outlived all of her husbands, Fran's outlived a lot of them. She wears two large gold rings, masses of melted gold heavily studded with diamonds. They began as wedding rings from two of her five marriages.

"I just added diamonds from other wedding rings, so now I have two rings instead of five!" she said. "Sometimes people admire my rings, and I just tell them if you've been married a lot of times, it gives you a lot to work with.

"Now I look on it as kind of a joke, but before I didn't even want to say I'd been married and divorced, it was so embarrassing, and here I'm supposed to be a good Catholic.

"I've been married a total of twelve and a half years. That's not much. My mom and dad were married for fifty-five years—and fought all the time! If that's happiness in marriage, forget it. I always said 'Not me.' So I went totally the other way. The instant something goes wrong, that's it.

"When I was young, my mom and dad didn't want me to get into trouble, but they didn't tell me what kind of trouble. They were very conservative, and I didn't learn anything about the birds and the bees.

"I was very, very shy. I remember a boy untied the bow on my dirndl dress, something else my German immigrant mom made me wear, like they did in Europe. I turned around and said, 'Quit it,' and I got my mouth taped because I talked in class. And I had my mouth taped the rest of the day, during recess and potty breaks and everything. Things like that just made growing up that much worse.

"When I was in high school, health education was eating the right vegetables, brushing your teeth, and taking some exercise. Nobody talked about sex, it was all hush-hush. I had no idea that there was such a thing as a menstrual period. No idea.

"One day, when I was about sixteen, it happened. I thought, 'Oh God, I'm sick,' but I didn't want to tell anybody. So I'd use my ankle socks, and they'd get bloody and fall on the hall floor. I had no idea there was such a thing as sanitary napkins. This went on for about three months. I'd just throw the socks in the garbage can. And my mom chewed me out because I was going through so many socks, but I didn't want to tell her, because I thought there was something wrong. I went through hell for about three months, with bloody skirts and everything.

"Finally, I went to the school nurse, and she told me what was going on. I couldn't believe it. I even thought at one time that if you kissed a guy, you get pregnant. You really should be told those things, look how embarrassing it was for me. So after I was married and had Mike and Joe, I said, 'These boys are going to know about the birds and the bees.' But I never did tell my mom.

"Then our name was so dumb—'Pfulg.' I said to myself, the instant I can get married, the first guy that says 'I love you,' I'm getting married. I'm gonna change this name."

Fran would make five attempts to change her name by this method, finally settling on the easily spelled and pronounced "Tate."

"I didn't have my first date until college," she said. "I finally got a date to a dance, so I went out and bought a dress, and it was a cotton dress, gray, green, and white stripes with puff sleeves and ruffles, and when I got to the dance, everyone else was in long strapless gowns with sequins. I look back now and think, 'Boy, I was stupid.'

"I was about the last one in my high school class to get married. During the war, a lot of girls got married because the guy was going into the service and they were afraid something would happen.

"I had a couple girlfriends who went overseas and met some colonels and captains, and I blamed my mom because I couldn't go overseas and find a colonel or a captain and I got what was left over on the home front. I tried to get a job in Civil Service and I passed the test, but as

LOVE AND MARRIAGES

soon as they realized my mom was from Germany and wasn't a citizen, they wouldn't let me leave the country.

"But that's why I think I got married in the first place, everyone else was getting married.

"During college, I worked up at the Mt. Baker Ski Lodge. I would take off the winter quarter around Christmas vacation and work as a waitress in the ski lodge, and that would give me money to go to school the rest of the year. That's where I met my first husband. He was a cook."

His last name was France, and their marriage eliminated the embarrassing "Pfulg" and gave her the rather theatrical name, Frances France. The marriage lasted only a short time.

Fran's husband became a steward in the merchant marine. Once she went on board to visit him when the ship was docked in Seattle. The ship, which carried mostly cargo and only a handful of passengers, sounded a horn an hour before sailing. Fran and her husband and a group of sailors who were musicians were down in the ship, playing and singing and making too much noise to hear the horn. When they heard the second horn, indicating 'all ashore who are going ashore,' they lingered, thinking it was only the first warning. When Fran tried to leave the ship, she found that it was already underway.

The ship went a short distance to Tacoma to pick up flour from the mill, but since there were no passengers boarding or leaving, Fran still couldn't get off. From

Tacos on the Tundra

Tacoma, the ship sailed to Ventura, California. Fran stayed hidden in the fo'c'sle for several days, with the crew slipping meals down to her. She mingled with the other passengers at Ventura, got off the ship and then rode a Greyhound bus back to Seattle.

Fran got to know many of her husband's friends, many of them sailors like himself.

"We would go into a restaurant, and he would bring a guy or two to our table, and they would entertain me while he went off with another guy," she said. "These guys were all nice to me, and they always brought me gifts—a pair of white silk pajamas from Japan, a gold nugget watch from Alaska, gifts from all over the world.

"But I didn't realize what was going on until one day I looked for him and one of his seaman friends said, 'Don't say I told you, but if you really want to know, go to…' and he named this hotel.

"So I went up this dingy, narrow staircase, like in a 1930s movie. At the top of the stairs was this little old weasel of a man sitting at the desk. I asked if my husband was there, and he told me the room number, but he said, 'You better knock first.' So I thought maybe he was with some girl. I knocked a couple times and then opened the door.

"He was with another guy.

"Now I look back and I see things that, if I had the knowledge I have now, I would have known. But I was really dumb—very naive. He even took me to gay bars, and I didn't recognize that at all. I saw guys holding hands and just thought they were good friends.

"And I had had a big, beautiful Catholic wedding, but that ended it."

The marriage was finally annulled, after the divorce.

"First they booted me out (of the Catholic Church) and wouldn't let me come to church, and then as soon as the marriage was annulled, they said I could come back. But at the same time, Alberto Rosellini and Ingrid Bergman had twin girls out of wedlock, and the Vatican overlooked that. I asked my priest if maybe I didn't have enough money to pay my way out of my situation, and he didn't like that.

"I got married again in 1953. What a jerk. He was about three inches shorter than I was. He was the son of friends of my parents. His dad was a woodcutter, too, like my dad. Since neither of us were married, they all thought he would be a good guy for me.

"But he just didn't know how to work. We were married just long enough to have two kids, Mike and Joe, and he probably worked six months out of that time. He used to go down to the dump with a brother-in-law that didn't know how to work either, and the two of them would shoot rats at the dump all day! Or he'd go fishing. I was working for the oil company then, and I'd be paying a babysitter while he was out shooting rats or fishing."

When Joe was born, Fran made the paper under the headline, "Busy mom has baby on the weekend." Joe was born at 4 p.m. Sunday, Fran left the hospital at midnight and she was back at work the next morning. An older couple who lived next door to her took care of the two children, but her husband's lack of ambition bothered the energetic Fran.

"One night I fixed fish for dinner, and he didn't come home at five, six, seven, eight…about ten o'clock I just put all his clothes and belongings out on the front porch with his dinner—a plate with fish on it and a potato. And a note: 'Don't bother to come in.' Of course, about midnight he came pounding on the door, but I just said, 'That's it! I'm done! No more!'

"And he was yelling, 'I can't live without you, I'm gonna shoot myself!' Then I remembered, I forgot to put out his gun, so I got it and threw it out the door, too. So that ended that."

Shortly after her second marriage ended, her junior high school principal met her crossing the main street in Auburn.

"I was about twenty-six years old then," she said. "He told me that I'd been successful at everything I'd done in my life, except in my choice in men. I never forgot that."

For twelve years, Fran worked her way up in the oil company. In 1965, the 41-year-old owner of the business suddenly and unexpectedly died of a heart attack while skiing. He had left instructions in his will that Fran become the general manager of the company.

The vice-president of the local bank questioned this arrangement, although the owner's widow assured him that

LOVE AND MARRIAGES

Fran knew the business better than anyone. He was also concerned about the demands of family life. Fran wrote to him, saying, "I know my capacity and I truly believe the keyed-up pace I keep both here at the office and with my active boys is the 'medicine' that keeps my heart ticking. I have been this way all my life; please do not ask me to change." She conceded that "seventy-five to eighty hours a week is a heavy schedule, but in our business we strive to give the best to everyone and I love being a part of it."

Fran went on to triple the size of the business, managing 2,500 oil accounts and 32 service station contracts and "making more money that I am now."

Meanwhile, she married again.

"I married a guy named Schults; that's why Mike and Joe go by 'Schults,' because he adopted them. He was about ten or twelve years younger than me. I was a Mobil Oil distributor and he ran one of the Mobil stations. He was a big guy, about six feet tall. He spent all his money gambling, but I didn't know it. He would always have expenses—he'd never come home with money. I was making good money, so here I was, still the breadwinner. Then I found out that he was wining and dining women and gambling.

"One Sunday he said he had some work to do at the station, so I decided to take the kids for a ride. We went up to Black Diamond, which was little, teeny-weeny, tiny town up in the hills, but they had a drive-in restaurant that sold foot-long hot dogs with peanut butter on them. Mike and

Joe-Joe were in the back seat leaning over my shoulder, and they said, 'Mama, that looks like our car coming.' And it was my car, and him in it with his arm around some girl, up in this backwoods town. So when he got home, his clothes were sitting out on the back porch. And that was the end of that."

Fran became active in many civic and professional organizations, in some of which she was the only female member. "It was all 500 men and me in Spokane at an Oil Heat Institute convention," she said. She was also the only "girl" in the Northwest Mobil Marketers.

The organizers of the conventions assumed that the head of an oil business would be a man who would bring along his wife; she would attend special teas and fashion shows. The registration forms were divided into two columns, for "men" and "ladies." On one of them, Fran wrote: "I am 'The Boss' and I go to the men's sessions. In the past, I registered as a 'man' and they refunded my money, so this year I registered as a 'lady'—OK?"

She addressed a discussion topic "Can a woman be successful and still be a lady?" in the following way:

"Through the past three and a half years (since the death of the owner of the business), I have stood right up to the men and will challenge any of them to a discussion on fuel oil, gasoline, and automotive products, and I have a bargaining pencil just as sharp as theirs."

She modestly concluded, "With all this in mind, someday I hope to be a successful businesswoman."

LOVE AND MARRIAGES

Then came Mr. Tate.

At the same time Fran was running the oil business, she began to give motivational talks, working with a Texas-based company called Success Motivation Institute. She conducted motivational seminars for high schools, colleges, treatment centers, prisons, and businesses. "I was really good at that," she said. "I can get people all fired up."

One of her jobs with Success Motivation Institute was at McNeil Island federal penitentiary. Her presentation was part of a big event for the prison, featuring W. Clement Stone (owner of the Combined Insurance Company of America) as a guest speaker, and with entertainment provided by the Fifth Dimension. Fran sat on a panel of twelve, including five model prisoners.

"They were a pretty enthusiastic crowd," Fran said. "Of course, in a prison, if you're a blonde girl, they're pretty enthusiastic anyway. It didn't matter what I said, I could have said, 'You're all a bunch of nitwits,' and they would have agreed."

One of the prisoners was a tall, well-spoken, handsome black man named Rory Tate, in jail for armed robbery of a San Francisco state bank. Like many of the prisoners that heard one of her talks, he began writing to Fran.

One day Fran went back to the prison to visit Tate. They fell in love.

"He could just melt a girl down," Fran said. "He had fascinating eyes.

"I was the one that got him out of prison. I was the key factor. I didn't need money, all I wanted was companionship. I was determined that it was going to work, but I just had to learn the hard way. He was a conniver and I got connived.

"It could have been the marriage of the century," she said. "We could have had the world by the tail. He was a great speaker, very eloquent. We were a perfect team. Neither of us saw color. It blew people's minds that we got along so well."

They formed Tate Enterprises, a business name that Fran has continued to use. They traveled "all over," giving motivational seminars.

"Prisoners usually don't know how to deal with reality," she said. "They talk about getting out of prison and making $50,000 a year. That's easy to say, but that's why they're in prison, because they try to do things the easy way. They've got all kinds of con ideas, and they think they can get money for nothing. They've got to realize that they're going to get out of prison with about $40 and a suit of clothes. You take a guy who's been in prison for ten years, he don't even know the price of bread. He has no idea what's happening in the real world." The goal of the motivational seminar was to help the inmates understand that they needed to take advantage of the job training available in prison, and that they had to think about what they were doing with their lives.

The ideas presented in the seminars—setting goals,

believing in oneself, handling discouragement—were not new, but Fran and Rory were received enthusiastically. A visiting reporter wrote, "Mrs. Tate bounded to the stage in answer to the audience's cheers. A vivacious and enthusiastic person, she stated she believed in 'a life full of living.'" A high school teacher said, "The Tates are great. How do you hold twenty-two students spellbound?" And a prison inmate wrote, "No one else could do what Fran and Rory have done for this group."

They worked with inmates of the Purdy Treatment Center for Women, an experimental minimum security facility described as an "open campus." The Tates worked intensively with groups of women to prepare them for a life after prison. Using her connections with local businesses, Fran worked to get donations of cosmetics, shoes, and clothing for the inmates. She drove them to job interviews and took them car shopping. She arranged for ten of them to have dinner in Seattle's Space Needle, escorted by members of the Junior Chamber of Commerce.

When Frank Sinatra, Jr. and his band played at a Seattle club, Fran decided to ask them to come to the prison.

"Rory said I'd never pull it off, that I could never get him to come and play," Fran said. "But I just put on my sexiest dress and went down to the club. First I talked to Sinatra's road manager, up in the light booth, and he practically threw me out. But then the club owner's son, who kind of had a crush on me, said, 'Go out in the alley and talk to him there when he goes out for a smoke.'"

Tacos on the Tundra

Sinatra and his 9-piece band agreed to play at the prison the following afternoon. After the show, the singer signed autographs, some of them in unusual places, like on sweatshirts and tennis shoes.

Before the show, Fran told the audience, "It just goes to show what we've been talking about in class—if you think you can do it, you can."

After the women were released from prison, Fran continued to work with them, helping them find jobs and apartments, taking them groceries and clothes, and trying to keep them out of further trouble with the police.

"I helped get a hooker who had killed her pimp out of prison," Fran said. "I worked real hard with her. She was good-looking and had studied ballet, but she started hooking when she was sixteen. She said she always wanted to be a model, so I got her in a training program with a big modeling school in Seattle. She married a guy who owned a big restaurant, but she couldn't stop hooking. It had been her life for so long. She would go out at night while he was at the restaurant, and then she'd come back home.

"Well, a hooker's not always in good company and sometimes she'd get beat up. She'd catch a cab in Seattle and come to my house, which at that time was about a $60 cab bill. Then I'd have to call her husband and say, 'Don't kick her out, she's trying.' But she just couldn't quit.

"One day I sat her down and asked her what it was about hooking that she just couldn't quit. Well, it was the money. She said she could make $300 in fifteen minutes.

She went to a big hotel near the airport where Japanese businessmen stayed and she'd pick up two or three of them a night.

"I said to her, 'All these years, I've been giving it away. Tonight, I'm coming with you. If you can make $300 in fifteen minutes, so can I.'

"We went to the hotel and were sitting there, having a drink, and here came three Japanese businessmen and they sat at a table next to us. We were both blondes, so they're looking at us. One of them came over and she went off with him, saying, 'I'll see you in a bit.' And here came another guy over to me.

"I don't know what it is, but—I couldn't do it. I headed for the bathroom just as fast as I could. She came back with her $300 and said, 'Did you go?' but I just couldn't. She sat down and waited for the next one. She didn't treat it as love or affection. It was a job. But I just couldn't do it."

Perhaps living in this environment of crisis and hard luck kept Fran from admitting the increasingly destructive nature of her relationship with her husband. Perhaps—sold on her own motivational message—she felt that it was up to her to make everything right. After all, every day she was telling her audiences, "You are what your thoughts make you."

To the rest of the world, their lives were a success. The Tates became divisional managers for Success Motivation and continued to give seminars.

"We were talking about this stuff so much, I was getting even more fired up," Fran said. "I guess I was my own best customer.

"They liked both of us," she said, "but my talks had more believability because I just shot from the hip, and he was putting on airs. He was a beautiful speaker, but for the actual message the audience stayed with me more because I actually practiced what I preached. I was just being Fran. And he was kind of faking it. How can you just come out of prison, start wearing a three-piece suit and carrying a briefcase, and talk about success when you've only been at it a year or two?"

Fran found that Tate had trouble letting go of his past life. His former associates couldn't accept his three-piece suits, briefcase and monogamous life.

"And because he wasn't that strong, he would vacillate and go off with them for some stupid thing," Fran said. "And then he'd be very mean when I caught him at it, because he thought he was slick. But criminals are stupid to begin with, that's how they end up in jail—because they think they won't get caught. But I would catch him at every stupid trick he did, and that would really burn him up. So then I'd get beat."

Tate turned out to be an abusive man. "One time I was only in pantyhose and a bra, and he chased me down the street with a gun. He almost killed me once with an ironing cord around my neck. I finally said, 'I'm not going to get beat no more.'

"His mom, who was a schoolteacher, used to chew him out. She always said I was too good for him. She'd say, 'He's rotten! You're too good for him!' I loved his mom. She was only fifteen years older than him—she was younger than me! She played the organ in the Catholic church, and in her own church, the Baptist church."

"But the boys loved him, everybody loved him, he was just a great guy."

Fran's oldest son, Mike, tells a slightly different story.

"He wasn't out of prison a month and he was dealing drugs," he said. "It was a trying time, to say the least. My mom was getting beat up by him. One time I was on the phone to call the cops and suddenly there was a gun stuck at my head. He said, 'Go ahead, dial the number. You'll die.' I was just a junior in high school.

"She had it pretty tough, but she was afraid to get rid of him for fear that he'd kill her.

"They used to fight all the time. He'd pound her, beat her. It was horrible. But she survived that. One of her problems was she could never find a husband who could keep up with her."

Part of the Success Motivation package was a self-evaluation form for personal goals and barriers to achieving them. Under "personal goals" Fran wrote, "To have a happy married life like many others." Under "barriers" she wrote, "I only wish I knew! Choose men of wrong caliber, I guess." Under "solutions" she wrote, "I've tried everything—what next?"

Tate went back to jail, and Fran's first trip to Barrow in 1970 may have been motivated in part by a desire to escape the situation. But she stayed in touch with his parole officer, who one day said, "I think he can make it, if you can handle it." She replied, "If he can make it, I can handle it." Tate followed Fran to Barrow and stayed about a year.

He was hired by the school district, a new organization formed after the North Slope Borough took over control of the schools from the Bureau of Indian Affairs. Tate became their public relations man.

"A perfect job for a smooth-talking con man," Fran said. "They loved him."

Fran and Rory accompanied 34 Iñupiat students on what had to have been the ultimate class trip. For 78 days, they traveled by bus across the country, making stops in Disneyland, Las Vegas, Nashville, Washington, D.C., New York City, and Montreal. In Juneau, they met Governor Jay Hammond.

Four of the students were sent back early in the trip for bad behavior.

"Two of them got drunk right there in the Holiday Inn in Los Angeles," Fran said. "After we got rid of some of the worst ones, the rest of them found out that we meant business."

Fran handled the finances for the trip.

"I doled out the money. If they were good, they might get some extra spending money, so I didn't have much trouble with them.

"But some of the kids that were from the villages didn't know how to take showers, use deodorant, comb their hair. When we got to Washington (state), I went out and bought them all a set of toiletries, shampoo, deodorant, toothpaste, and then showed them how to use them."

Life in Barrow did not improve the Tates' relationship and they were divorced in 1974.

For the next fifteen years, Tate tried to reestablish contact with Fran.

"He sent me letters saying he needed $40,000. He'd say, 'Don't ask what it's for, I've finally learned how to put a proposal together, and I'll pay you back just as soon as I get the money.'" She never answered the letters.

"He would call, saying, 'I think about you all the time. We've got to get back together.'"

Once Fran replied, "I think about you, too. When I'm in the shower."

Why in the shower?

"Because that's when I can see the scars."

"He just couldn't do anything without conniving, trying to get big money the easy way," Fran said.

"I kept the name 'Tate' because it's a catchy name, easy to remember, easy to write. But I always laugh, sometimes tourists will have the same name and they'll ask, 'Where does your family come from?' I say, 'Well, probably not where yours came from.'"

All of Fran's husbands were younger than her, and three

of them are now dead. The first husband was killed in a fight, Schults died of a heart attack and the second husband, her sons' father, died of cancer. He contacted Fran and asked to see the boys before he died.

"Mike said, 'Where the hell's he been for the last thirty years? He don't need to see me now, he never missed me before.'"

On the wall of Fran's office is a greeting card. The outside of the card says, "Marriage is like a tug of war." Inside the card says, "One big jerk after another."

"I'll never get married again. But the thing I miss most is—I love to dance. I just want to dance. But if you ask a guy for a dance, they don't want to end it with just a dance. They want to cling forever. So I quit doing it. But I can't hardly sit still with good music playing.

"Everyone asks how I can travel alone. I do fine. In fact, after I see people at the restaurant all day, I'd just as soon be alone.

"I've only been married a total of twelve and a half years," she said. "That's not very much, when you think about it."

Years later in Barrow, Fran would make one more attempt at marriage.

CHAPTER 5
The Original Pepe

Fran was living in Renton, Washington in 1968, following a grueling work schedule that was a pattern for most of her life. She was an engineering draftsman during the day, worked as a cocktail waitress from 11 p.m. until 7 a.m., and squeezed in some seminars for Success Motivation Institute.

"I slept very little," she said. "I'd lean against the wall." The bar where she worked was in a Sheraton Hotel, near Long Acres Race Track. Its decor followed a horse racing theme, and the waitresses wore little jockey outfits with red jackets, caps, and short shorts. In those days, sexual harassment was a part of business.

"Whether or not you were a good waitress, you always got a tip if you had good legs," Fran said. "In fact, in order to be a waitress, the owner would take you up to his office and you had to put on one of the outfits and walk back and forth, and if your legs were good enough, you got to be a waitress. Fortunately, my legs are better looking than my face, so I got the job. I was about forty, and I beat out a lot of younger girls.

"It was the first time I'd ever done any cocktail waitressing. When I was a little girl, I'd hear my mom say, 'She's just a cocktail waitress.' I'll tell you, the cocktail waitress has to be one of the smartest women in the world. You take an order of drinks around the table, and you might have ten or twelve to a table, but when you give it to the bartender, you have to give it a different way. First the 'straights,' then 'on the rocks,' then the blends, mixes, highballs, wine, and beer is last. And that's how the bartender gives it back to you. Then when you get back to the table, you have to remember how they ordered it. And if these twelve guys say, 'Another round,' you can't go back and ask them all over again. I learned real quick that someone is not 'just a cocktail waitress.'"

The establishment's bartender had a boyfriend who owned a restaurant called Pepe's Mexican Villa. Every evening after closing his own restaurant, he came to the Sheraton to eat dinner with his girlfriend.

"He was a real joker," Fran said, "but I didn't know this at first. One day he asked me, 'Do you have oysters on your menu today?' When I said yes, he said, 'Are they male or female?' I said I didn't know there was a difference. He said, 'Oh yes, I don't like the male oysters, the female ones are much softer. Why don't you go ask the cook?' And I thought, 'I never heard of that. I've been a waitress a long

The Original Pepe

time, but I never knew about the oysters.' So I went and asked the cook, not knowing that the cook was in on it. This wasn't the first time that Pepe had pulled this. The cook opened the refrigerator and said, 'No, we just have male oysters today. See, we have to keep them separate.' And it was a double door refrigerator, so he showed me the two sides.

"I went back to Pepe and told him we only had male oysters that day. He said, 'Are you sure?' and I said, 'Yes, I saw him open the refrigerator, he keeps the males on one side and the females on the other.' And then I said, 'You know, I never knew that before. I've worked in a lot of restaurants and nobody ever asked me if the oysters were male or female.' He pointed to some other customers and said, 'You see those guys over there? Ask them; they're in the seafood wholesale business.'

"So I went over and started asking them about the difference between male and female oysters, since they were in the seafood wholesale business, and one of them finally said, 'We're in the seafood wholesale business? I'm an insurance agent and he's with a realty company.' I looked over at Pepe and that son-of-a-gun was laughing."

Fran told that story after she came to Barrow. When she started working on the drilling sites, the workers gave her a CB radio and a call name—Oyster Girl.

"I also got the nickname 'Pancha' when I was working at Pepe's. It's Spanish for Fran. I answer almost quicker to Pancha than to Fran.

"One night, Pepe said, 'You know, we need a waitress like you over at my restaurant. You could make good tips anywhere, come over and see me.' I went to check it out, and it was a neat little place. I'd never worked in a Mexican restaurant, and he seemed like a nice guy. His name was Bob Worthington, but everybody called him Pepe. His mother was Mexican and his father was English, but Pepe looked all Mexican. He was a big guy who sat in the corner and drank sangria all day. He'd say, 'Honey, fill my glass.' He wasn't like me, working. He just sat in the corner. From his corner, he could watch the waitresses and the customers in all the sections.

"I went to work for him, and later on, when I decided to stay in Barrow and was thinking about opening a restaurant, I called him and asked if he wanted to go in partners. But he said, 'Not up there.' I didn't know where to start with a restaurant, I didn't even know what you needed in the kitchen. He sent me a list of equipment, and I looked at it and saw 'cheese melter' and thought, 'What in the hell is a cheese melter?' Then I found out it cost about $1,000—to melt cheese!?"

After working for Pepe for two years, the engineering firm that she worked for sent her up to Barrow. She quit the restaurant, but assured them that she'd only be gone for six months.

"When I come back, can I have my old job back?" she asked.

On June 23, 1970, two weeks before her trip to Alaska,

The Original Pepe

Fran and her sons took a trip to Tijuana, Mexico. She has a souvenir photo of the three of them sitting in a cart pulled by a donkey. All three are wearing big sombreros. The caption on the card says, "If you don't like the photo, blame the jackass."

Chapter 6
The Age of Aquarius

"When I worked at the Sheraton," Fran said, "every now and then someone would ask, 'Are you a Libra? I can just tell you're a Libra.' When I asked them what that meant, they'd say something like, 'Oh, you're in love with love.'"

In 1970, a few months before her first trip to Barrow, Fran had her astrological chart done by Mr. H.E. Schubert, a Seattle astrologer.

Of the sun-in-Libra and moon-in-Scorpio combination, Mr. Schubert had this to say:

"Independence of mind and action, thought and expression are the outstanding traits of your nature. You are quick mentally with a penetrating and absorbing curiosity. You make rapid strides in the world and are stamped with a keen ambition, the following of which is an intimate need with you.

"You're not without your peculiar kind of tact, but you despise a pussy footer or a kowtower and will say so to his face if the opportunity arises.

"Emotionally you are ardent and intense, and although you think of yourself as being self-sufficient, you really are not at all and do best when you've settled your emotional life by having someone around you to balance your enthusiasms, although you would probably hoot at the idea that you need anyone at all."

Schubert then turned to the relationship of the planets to each other. Since Uranus squares with the sun, he noted that "eccentricity is increased, an irascible nature but with an inspirational quality that gets forgiveness from the world."

He also said, "You have been dejected, depressed and discouraged; probably you've had your share of unconventional and erratic love affairs. As you grow older, you turn from egocentric to humanitarian, interested in large ideas, large groups of people and social problems on a large scale."

The conjunction of Mercury with Mars, marked as "important" by the astrologer, brought this analysis: "You have a quick, brilliant mind, a sharp, penetrating insight, and grasp of mathematical and scientific intricacies. You also have an abrupt manner of speech, not marked by diplomacy. You speak your mind and can make trouble for yourself. You are contentious, loving a good argument."

In analyzing the triangular relationship of Mars to

Venus he said: "You probably were born to a good social status—or if not, you are a lucky child who rises far above your original social status. It is one of the positions of material luck and always keeps you from the worst degrees of want. You can make a little go a long way if you have to.

"You have a good insight and a good business head, not easily deceived. You're utterly honest and trustworthy, a stickler for duty and the sanctity of obligations.

"You are a builder, willing to start at the bottom of a career and work your way deliberately to the top. There's nothing flimsy about the structure you build. This may make you an actual architect, or it may make you figuratively an architect of your own fate, laying your plans far in advance and working soundly for their accomplishment. Your judgement is excellent and you always know where you are going and how each brick will fit in the eventual product."

Fran wrote Schubert a letter thanking him for doing her chart. "This is very interesting," she said. "One thing that I noticed, and it did leave me in a state of wonderment, was that my past life has certainly been patterned in an almost identical fashion as the horoscope reads. I may even become a believer of this material."

If she could have seen where the future would soon take her, her state of wonderment would have been even greater.

The Age of Aquarius

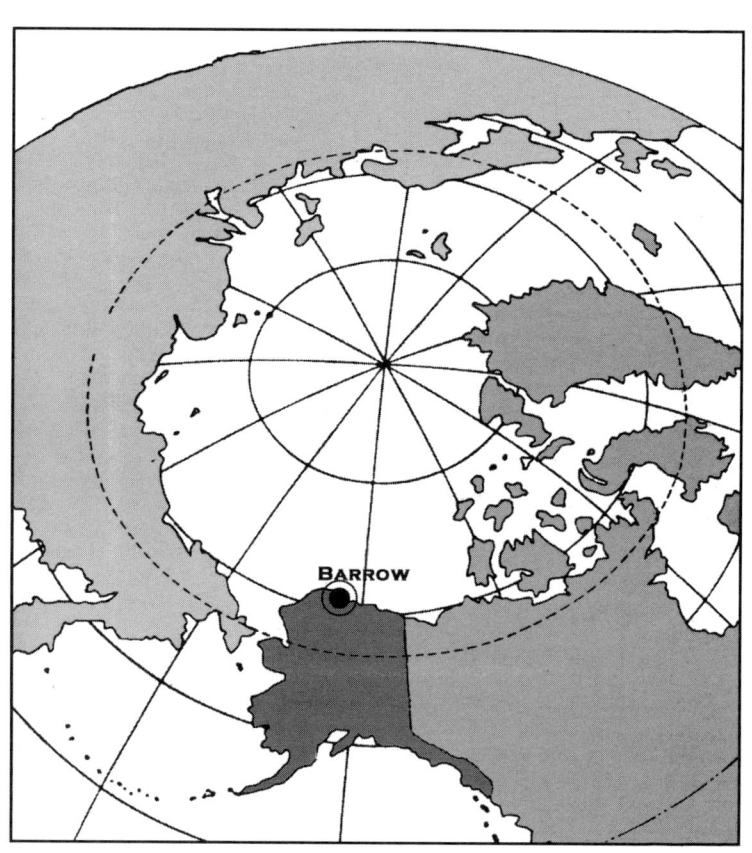

CHAPTER 7
The Spy Who Came into the Cold

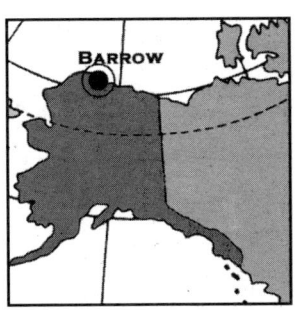

"I first came up here July 4, 1970," Fran said. "I arrived on a Wien Air flight, an F27. We left Anchorage about six a.m. and got here about eleven in the morning and, at that time, Wien Air only gave you peanuts and a can of tomato juice.

"There were about sixteen passengers, and the rest of the plane was filled with cargo. Next to me was a fifty-five-gallon drum of oil.

"The Wien terminal was about as big as two box cars put together. About ten people could stand inside, shoulder to shoulder. They just brought your luggage over on a forklift and threw it on the ground. It didn't come in on a conveyor belt—it didn't even come into the building! I remember somebody brought up fishing poles that day, and they were all broken because they just threw everything. You just picked up whatever was yours.

"It was the early 1970s, so I was wearing a miniskirt, a

black and white herringbone tweed skirt and vest and a black turtleneck and high black boots. There had been some trouble with hookers over at Prudhoe Bay, so everybody was looking at me, like they thought maybe one of them had drifted over here.

"It was the Fourth of July and there had been a big storm, and the ice was all pushed up on the beach. At that time the beach was farther out, but the road out there was washed out by the storm, so the two guys that came to pick me up at the airport came in a D8 Cat, a front-end loader."

Fran had made her first trip to Alaska the previous year, going to Anchorage for an oil convention, one of the highlights of which was a wild game buffet featuring moose, seal liver, and maktak.

But she came to Barrow as a sort of corporate spy, investigating a branch operation of her employer, Pacific Architects and Engineers. Wearing a wig and disguised "as a dumb blonde secretary," she set out to uncover incompetence and corruption.

"There was a big refrigerator in the project manager's office, but it wasn't for food," she said. "Ten o'clock every morning and three o'clock every afternoon certain VIPs would walk in with their briefcases and they would have a meeting. I couldn't figure out why they needed a meeting every day at three o'clock.

"So I got kind of cozy with one of these guys. I saw that every night he took a briefcase home, and every morning he came to work with one. I was doing all the work, so I knew there must be something going on. So when he went in to his morning meeting, I opened up his briefcase and there were two bottles of liquor. I closed it and didn't say anything.

"Then one day, they invited me to one of their afternoon meetings. They would just sit there from three until seven in the evening and just drink. There was a head secretary whose name was Bonnie—'whatever Bonnie wants, Bonnie gets,' they'd say. She had so much information on them, she got whatever she wanted—her house, jewelry, anything.

"They used to have meetings in another room with a guy named Pat, and my boss would go over there in the afternoons. They had a wall furnace there, so I put my typewriter next to it, saying 'It's too cold over there, I'm going to sit over here by the heater.' You could hear everything through that heater. I would sit there doing statistical typing, just numbers, a job I really hated, but I would listen. Oh man, what would go on in there! They were just goofing off and ripping off the company, not getting the work done, people getting paid for work they weren't even doing.

"The big boss, Ed Shay, came up from the head office in Los Angeles. They had told me what files to look for, and to tell them where to find them, and he just walked in one day with an entourage of department heads and they just cleaned house. About eleven people got fired that day.

Some of them figured out that it must have been me, so Bonnie quickly typed up a complaint that I was the worst employee they'd ever had, but of course Ed Shay got rid of that."

Most of the non-Native population at the time lived several miles north of Barrow at NARL, the Naval Arctic Research Lab. Construction had begun near the end of World War II and continued over the next two decades. At the time of Fran's arrival, the accumulation of Quonset huts and other buildings made a community larger than Barrow itself. NARL served as a base camp for oil exploration and as housing and laboratory space for hundreds of scientists who came to study arctic climate, vegetation and wildlife.

"I lived out there at NARL—we called it 'the camp,'" Fran said. "It was dormitories, men's and women's, but you'd never know the difference, there were as many men in the women's dorm all the time as women. That really bugged me because they had a community shower with three stalls but no curtain. The door had louvers on it, and they pointed down, so I could stand in the shower and look out and see big, hairy feet going by.

"It got so bad that instead of staying in the dormitory, I went over to the office. I put my sleeping bag on the big table that we had for the blueprints and slept there.

"The people who worked and stayed at the camp were divorced from Barrow, they didn't really have anything to do with Barrow at all. There was the DEW Line, the Air

Force, the Navy. You lived there, worked there, ate there. There was a bar with a jukebox and dancing, out at the DEW Line station. There was a movie theater. It was a separate community."

Construction of the DEW Line (Distant Early Warning) began in 1952 in response to the Cold War threat of Soviet air attack over the North Pole. A line of radar scanning stations was built across the Arctic in just three years. This massive construction project brought a large influx of people from the outside to northern Alaska. The early crews at the stations tended to have a negative influence on the nearby communities, as they brought in alcohol and had little positive interaction with local residents.

"But that's how I got here," Fran said. "Then I was assigned permanently, still with Pacific Architects and Engineers. But I wasn't doing engineering work, so I went over to PET 4 (Naval Petroleum Reserve Number 4) and worked under Commander Shaffer."

Natives of the North Slope had long been aware of oil coming from the ground, and early explorers in the area mention Natives using chunks of oil-soaked sod as fuel. Charles Brower, Barrow's first permanent white resident, first described oil in the Prudhoe Bay area. It was discovered in 1886, when Brower and a companion went ashore to hunt caribou during an unsuccessful search for whales in the Beaufort Sea east of Barrow. In his autobiography, *Fifty Years Below Zero*, Brower wrote, "A small lake spread out before us, its water curiously dark and ranging from a liquid center to an asphalt-like substance around the edge." When they put a match to it, they discovered that it burned.

A 37,000-square mile area in arctic Alaska was originally set aside for oil exploration in 1923. During World War II these reserves were developed as part of the fuel needs for the Pacific operations.

On December 26, 1967, after drilling more than 13,000 feet without success, Exxon struck black gold. The oil deposit was the largest ever discovered in North America, and held an estimated 9.6 billion barrels of oil.

The Navy controlled the drilling contracts until 1976, when they were transferred to the Department of the Interior.

"I worked out there on the drilling sites in 1974, after I first came up here," Fran said. "I worked in the shake and shale room and as a roustabout. I didn't know anything about the oil fields, so when I had to draw something, like the rat hole or the derrick, I didn't understand how it worked. When you make a blueprint, you have to know what you're drawing. A rat hole is the place underground where they store the pipe that's needed on the derrick as they drill down. But I didn't know that.

"When you set up a new drilling site, the shale shack, the water room, the mess hall, the generators—everything has to be planned a certain way. I had to plan how the electric lines would come from the generator—everything. But I didn't know what I was drawing.

"I asked Commander Shaffer if I could go out on the drilling rigs and work there, so I could understand what I was drawing. First I had to get permission from the tool pusher—that's a nickname for the head foreman. I worked on rigs and did my engineering work on the side—I worked fifteen hours a day, and, man, I was tired.

"The first thing they had me do was work as a roustabout, a 'go-fer.' They had me carrying heavy pieces of equipment, chains, going around oiling equipment. Then I was in the shale shaker room where the geologists were. The core of the drill goes down in the ground, with a diamond drill bit. You have to keep the drill bit from going dry, so you slurry it—pour in a mixture of water, potassium and sulphur. They'd bring in hundred-pound sacks of the chemicals on a forklift. We had to lift them up to a hopper, open them up and pour them into it. You had to be careful that the hopper didn't get stuck, because the sulphur could blow back into your face and burn your eyes. I worked with a guy, lifting those hundred-pound sacks, and for every one he lifted, I lifted one, too.

"We'd get so dirty working in the shale shaker room. My face was just like I was wearing a mud pack. I worked like that on six different wells."

Charley Edwardsen, an Iñupiat man who drove a forklift on one of the rigs, remembered her performance in the hard environment.

"She is one tough lady," he said admiringly. "I never saw anybody that could work like that. She was lifting sacks that probably weighed as much as she did."

"I remember that first day when they opened the doors to bring in the forklift with the pallet of sacks," Fran said. "Charley got off the rig, looked up at me getting ready to unload those hundred-pound sacks and said, 'I can't believe my eyes. That's the damndest thing I ever seen.'

"Iko Bay was the hardest," Fran remembered. "It took us thirty-seven days to drill that hole, and for thirty-seven days I didn't take off my clothes to sleep. And there was a guy in the bunk below me who snored on the way in and on the way out. When we were out at Iko Bay, we never came into town, we just lived out there in little eight-by-ten shacks—they called them 'wanigans', two sets of bunk beds to a room. All we did was put down newspaper on the bunks, just laid down on lots of newspaper. No showers—we washed in a wash basin, and if you're the ninth one in line, you might as well not wash. I'd just lay down on the newspapers with my boots on. I can sleep anywhere, it didn't matter—except for the guy below me that kept boiling potatoes! It wouldn't have been so bad if he just snored one way, but he did it coming in and going out."

Photos of Fran from that time show a perky blonde in a red parka, usually surrounded by large, bearded guys. Her scrapbooks include many pictures of heavy equipment: rolligons (vehicles with huge ballooning tires that can cross the tundra without damaging it), man-hauls (a sort of freight car on tall wheels, used to move people from place to place), barges, and aircraft of all descriptions.

A photo of one of the drilling rigs that she worked on shows a primitive structure reminiscent of those in nineteenth-century photos of the Pennsylvania oil fields. The ultra technology of the modern pipeline era was still several years away.

"My last job with the Navy was out at Lonely. ("Lonely" is the nickname of a DEW Line station at Pitt Point, some 200 miles east of Barrow. The name itself gives a pretty good picture of the place.) I was the project manager out there. We put in a new runway lighting system and a new generator, and extended the runway, and I designed it and worked with the guys. I was back and forth out there from June until Thanksgiving Day, 1975. They had wanted us to stay until January.

"But that was one of the coldest years we ever had up here, and they had two men staying out at the camp, and those guys said, 'We ain't staying out here.' The only way to get water was to take that big Aardvark thing (a piece of equipment that looks like a boxcar on huge wheels, fitted with a tank, pump and hose, and used to haul water) and go out to the lake and pump out the water, and there were wolves out there and polar bears. Once a guy got eaten by a polar bear, right between two of the shacks that we lived in.

"So these two guys got on that plane that I came in on, and they left. When I got to the camp, I saw that the whole kitchen was flooded. The pipes had broken, and the whole kitchen was covered in ice. The whole place was cold.

"I had no phone, just a radio to call up to the DEW Line station. I took this rickety old truck and drove up there and I called Commander Woods. The guys (that had left) had just gotten in. It took them about an hour and fifteen minutes to fly to Barrow, and it took me about that long to figure I wasn't going to stay out there all by myself, just me and the polar bears!

"So I called him and told him what the situation was. He said, 'Fran, I am Commander Woods, and I am in the Navy, and in the Navy you do as you're told.' And I said, 'I'll tell you what, Commander Woods. My name is Fran Tate, and I am *not* in the Navy and I am getting the hell out of here whether you send a plane for me or not!' The guys on the DEW Line were listening in and just cracking up.

"A Twin Otter came in to take one of the DEW Line guys out, so I just jumped on that plane. I came back to Barrow and handed over the keys, and the camp stayed closed until January when the Department of the Interior took over."

When the Interior began overseeing the oil leases, Husky was one of the first companies to bid.

"Husky wanted to hire me, but they wanted to send me to their Anchorage office. I said, 'No, I think I like it up here.' That's when I started to look around Barrow to see what I could do."

THE SPY WHO CAME INTO THE COLD

Photo courtesy of North Slope Borough Iñupiat History, Language and Culture Commission.
Photo by Robert Stapleton

Chapter 8
Life at the Top of the World

There isn't much that Fran throws away. She has dozens of scrapbooks containing photographs and souvenirs from her first days in Barrow.

Human beings have lived at the Barrow town site since about 6,000 B.C. It is believed that the ancestors of the Iñupiat people crossed the Bering Sea, probably by boat, since the Bering land bridge, a 1000-mile-wide plain over which the ancestors of other Native Americans crossed from Asia, became submerged at the end of the last Ice Age.

During the winter, the Iñupiat traditionally lived in sod houses, made by cutting out blocks of sod and stacking them around the resulting depression. The walls rounded up to the top of the house, where a sort of skylight made from gut skin stretched on a wooden frame could be installed. This type of housing, in use for thousands of years, was judged unsanitary by late nineteenth and early twentieth century missionaries, who encouraged people to build frame houses. Charles Brower opposed this, remarking, "I knew they would not be as comfortable in a small frame house as they were in their own style igloos that had taken them centuries to develop."

One of Fran's photos, taken in 1976, shows a sod house standing in the middle of Barrow. Still occupied, it was a curiosity, and the other photos show that by then most of the residents had adopted other styles of housing. The photos also show blocks of freshwater ice stacked next to the houses, ready to be melted for drinking water.

Building materials (other than sod) have always been in short supply in this treeless environment, and over the years residents have constructed homes from connex boxes (shipping containers that look like small boxcars with no wheels), scrap lumber, and the remains of other buildings. When the hospital began to build new employee housing in 1993, it had to first remove a collection of Quonset huts and other makeshift structures—including a white wooden hospital building constructed in the 1930s—that had been gradually cobbled into cramped and drafty apartments. A long, narrow hallway snaked among the buildings, connecting them to the hospital. The buildings were auctioned off and hauled away. They can still be seen around Barrow, as can sections of the hallway.

At the other end of the architectural spectrum is the $4 million Stuaqpak or "big store," the Iñupiaq name for the Alaska Commercial Company. It was under construction at the time, and Fran's photograph shows the internal framework of the unusual curved front of the building. Even today its architecture is eye-catching, and in 1976 the building must have looked like it had been dropped from another planet.

Fran remembered another store, a small building where flour, sugar, and tea were scooped out of canvas sacks, weighed on scales, and sold by the pound. Old men sat at tables made from wooden cable spools and played checkers. "It reminded me of the places where my parents bought supplies back in the Depression," Fran said.

Living conditions in Barrow were still rather primitive in the early 1970s. For example, it wasn't until 1978 that the villages on the North Slope had telephone service, which began with one phone installed in each village. People who wanted to make a call had to wait in line or resort to short-wave radio. The village landing strips had no electric lights. During the winter (when there is little or no daylight), an incoming pilot would buzz the village, and someone would come out and place smudge pots along the runway so the plane could land.

Susanna Marquette, who moved to Barrow in the late 1970s, remembered her early days.

"The first year I was here I bought ice from an older Iñupiat man. Almost all the houses had blocks of ice stacked next to them. You had a barrel in the house for fresh water, and you'd just put in a block of ice when it got low.

"Like most households, we had a honey bucket in the corner with a curtain around it. It was basically a five-gallon plastic bucket, and you could buy a seat to go on top. The real fancy ones had a pipe that vented the fumes. You kept it sanitized with lots of Lysol. You could put it in the qanitchaq, and it would be frozen in the winter, so you wouldn't have any smell, but then you had the risk of getting stuck on the metal seat. The other problem was that if it got frozen, you couldn't get the contents out of the bucket, so then you had to either put it on the stove or in the room to warm up so it could be removed. There were lots of stories of someone carrying it out and having the whole thing spill on them. The sinks didn't have any drains, so you just threw dishwater or washwater outside.

"I remember the houses being oriented to footpaths rather than roads, and when the roads were first laid out in town, the houses were at odd angles relative to them."

The prosperity brought by the Alaska Native Claims Settlement Act and the development of the oil fields at Prudhoe Bay resulted in major civic improvements to Barrow and the other villages on the North Slope. These included new schools (like the $84 million high school), a public bus system (that drives around Barrow's estimated 45 miles of gravel roads), airport improvements and the Utilidor, a "corridor of utilities" in which water, gas, phone, and sewer lines run through nearly 4 miles of insulated underground tunnel to those houses and buildings that have paid to be hooked up to it.

Present-day Barrow looks like the sandbox of a kid with a lot of Tonka trucks, but it wasn't always like that.

"We didn't use to have all this fancy road equipment," Fran said. "Instead of hauling the snow away and putting it in a big pile near the ocean, like they do now, in the spring they'd dig a trench along both sides of the streets, running it down towards the ocean. So the snowmelt, the rain and trash and sewage would flow down in these trenches, and there was a lot of hepatitis.

"Our kids play in mud puddles now. They played in them then, only then they were poop puddles. In those days we didn't have honey bucket service where they come to your house and pick it up. You had a fifty-five-gallon drum that you filled up, sitting on a sled in front of your house.

"For a while the Borough tried to use garbage cans, thirty-gallon plastic garbage cans. That was a mess. They were hit, smashed, stolen, blown away by the wind. Then they finally settled on the fifty-five-gallon metal drums. You'd put one on a sled, and when it was full you'd hook it up to your car or snow machine and haul it off to the dump," Fran said.

"But sometimes between here and there is a long way. You could hit gravel or a bump, or the sled could get going too fast for the car or snow machine.

"Once I was going to the gas station, which used to be at the edge of Browerville. Ahead of me maybe two hundred or three hundred feet was a pickup truck, and coming across the tundra was a guy on a snow machine pulling a sled with two fifty-five-gallon drums strapped to it. I could see that he was going to cross the road in front of the pickup. I thought to myself, 'It looks like they're going to get to the same place at the same time.'

"The snow machine crossed the road, but there was about fifty feet of rope between it and the sled with the drums of poop on it. The pickup truck hit the rope and swung the sled around and it hit the truck broadside and a hundred gallons of poop went all over that pickup. The guy on the snow machine was jerked right off when the truck hit the rope. It was like a scene in a movie.

"Tommy Akootchook did the same thing. He was hauling a drum on a sled behind his snow machine, and he hit a bump alongside the road and his snow machine turned over. But the sled was still coming. It crashed into him and covered him and the snow machine. Those were some of the cute things that happened in the good old days."

The gas line, a metal pipe that is now underground through most of the town, used to rest about a foot and a half above the ground on metal drums that were sawed in half. One Barrow Apartments tenant came home drunk, tripped over the pipe and broke his leg. Fran, who was managing the apartments but had no vehicle, packed him on her back to the hospital.

"He was drunk, so he was just dead weight," Fran said. "And he was complaining the whole time because his leg hurt."

LIFE AT THE TOP OF THE WORLD

For many years, the private vehicular traffic of Barrow consisted of a few dozen pickup trucks.

"In about 1979, Whitlam Adams brought up the first car, a Ford LTD, and it was like President Kennedy driving down the street, everybody stopped and stared. It was a big four-door sedan, but it got smashed up after two or three weeks. I think it's still sitting there where it got smashed."

The town did not have a large selection of restaurants when Fran arrived in Barrow. Al's Cafe, a 16-by-20-foot rustic establishment, described by Fran as "a shack," stood in what is now Pepe's parking lot. Brower's Cafe operated in the old Point Barrow Refuge Station, a wooden building that was put up in 1889 as a shelter for stranded whalers. It's still in business, but was always open only for the summer tourist season.

Fran would have a few more irons in the Barrow fire before plunging into the restaurant business. Having turned down a job in Anchorage, Fran looked around for a way to survive in Barrow. Her first venture was a secretarial business.

"At that time, the women up here had a hard time getting to work. Partying came first, and they didn't have any alarm clocks, and they never showed up for work, so I was a sort of 'Kelly Girl.' I had a mag-card machine and a copy machine, a transcriber, a tape recorder. I called the business 'Speedy Secretary.' Some people still call me 'speedy secretary.' Sometimes I'd go to an office and work for them there all day, taking two or three girls' places, or they'd bring the work to my office—just a little hole in the wall—and I'd work all night, typing, doing minutes of meetings, resumes, reports—just everything."

This explosion in secretarial work was caused by the creation of corporations under the Alaska Native Claims Settlement Act. ANCSA probably had a greater effect on Bush Alaska that any other piece of legislation in history. To understand life in Barrow, a short explanation of it is needed.

Unlike Native people in the Lower 48, Alaska's Native people had never signed a treaty or been defeated in war. Although the U.S. government purchased Alaska from Russia in 1867, it did not hold clear title to the land.

Prudhoe Bay's vast deposits of oil were discovered in 1968. During the energy crisis of the early 1970s, there was pressure to develop Prudhoe Bay and to build the 800-mile trans-Alaska pipeline that would link the oil fields with the port of Valdez. Alaska's Native people viewed these developments with concern and feared that they would be denied the use of lands that they and their ancestors had occupied for centuries. They realized that they must take steps to preserve not only the land, but their way of life.

When the oil industry discovered that it could not build a pipeline on land whose ownership was not legally established, Native Alaskans found that the major oil companies were a strange ally in their struggle to settle land claims. Native groups organized, and, after lengthy negotiations,

President Richard Nixon signed the ANCSA into law on December 18, 1971. The Act provided for the establishment of twelve (later thirteen) regional Native corporations (roughly corresponding to tribal groups) and dozens of village corporations. These corporations divided a total of 44 million acres of land and $962 million in cash. About 70,000 Alaskan Natives were registered as corporation shareholders in the original Act.

The Iñupiat of the North Slope formed the Arctic Slope Regional Corporation, known as ASRC. The City of Barrow and the eight villages on the North Slope also formed village corporations. The members of this often confusing system of corporations became major employers in a region that had virtually no cash economy until the 1960s. Suddenly the Iñupiat found themselves moving from centuries of loose socialism to a capitalist economy.

The many corporations and organizations, each with its own acronym, make the political scene on the North Slope very confusing. For this book's purposes, the most important ones are the already mentioned ASRC and the North Slope Borough, which is the local governing body, the equivalent of a county government in the Lower 48. The North Slope Borough administers an area approximately the size of Minnesota, with a population of 8,000.

In an article about ANCSA published in *Alaska Magazine* in May 1977, Lael Morgan wrote, "There was little Alaskan expertise available (Native or white) for the creation of a dozen multi-million dollar businesses in

Tacos on the Tundra

1972."

"I worked for Arctic Slope Regional Corporation, the North Slope Borough, Utpeagvik Iñupiat Corporation, everybody," Fran said. "I had the first big IBM copier. But then everybody started to get copiers, they got new typewriters, the girls finally got alarm clocks, so the business started to dwindle. It was fun for two years, and I learned a lot about the Borough because I typed so many things. I did all the meetings and I had to buy a special ball for my typewriter with the extra Iñupiaq letters. I still have it."

At the same time she was being "Speedy Secretary," Fran was indirectly involved in a scandal at the Iñupiat University of the Arctic, a private institution created in 1975 and funded by the North Slope Borough. Its purpose was to provide adult education with a vocational emphasis. Fran worked as a clerk and part-time instructor, teaching some basic office management classes.

A man named Richard Ivey was the financial director for the newly-created Iñupiat University. The University of Alaska established an extension center in Barrow during the same year and hired Ivey as its director, without knowing of his connection with Iñupiat University.

The two schools—just to make things a bit more muddled—shared the same building.

Ivey and James D. Milne, the president of Iñupiat University, created what a journalist would later describe as an "imaginary university."

"I sat in the same office with Ivey, the guy who wrote

the grants," Fran said, "and he'd open the mail each day. Every time a check would come in, a green check from the state, I noticed that instead of it going into the bank deposit, he'd tuck it into his briefcase. I just wrote in my diary 'Something funny,' but of course I didn't know what was going on."

One day a woman phoned Iñupiat University and asked Fran if she had cashed her last check. Since Fran wasn't getting paid for the classes she was teaching, she asked the woman what she meant. The woman said, "For the classes you've been teaching in the village. Shorthand, bookkeeping…" Fran interrupted, "I don't even know shorthand! I'm not a bookkeeper! I don't know what you're talking about." The woman said, "Thank you, Fran" and hung up.

In the 35-page judgement handed down in 1981, Ivey was convicted of 26 charges related to his creation of the imaginary university. Sheila Toomey of the *Anchorage Daily News* had this to say: "Ivey invented a fall semester course schedule and listed six clerical employees of Iñupiat University as instructors. The clerks were unaware of Ivey's actions.

"He then fabricated registration records, using the names of students who had received tuition grants to Iñupiat University—apparently also without the students' knowledge.

"Ivey reported to the university that the non-existent instructors had taught the non-existent students a variety of courses ranging from shop work to comprehensive business English. He submitted fifteen end-of-semester grade reports with forged instructors' signatures."

Ivey intercepted more that $14,000 in payroll checks. He repeated his performance the following semester for another $12,000. At his trial, he offered this creative defense: Due to his innovative educational methods, the instructors did not realize that they had taught the courses.

He also felt that the instructors should not have been allowed to testify, since they didn't have the educational expertise to know whether or not they had been teaching the classes. Ivey was convicted of forgery and obtaining money by false pretenses.

"After the FBI came," Fran said, "they showed me the checks in my name that he had cashed. The signature wasn't even close!"

During the same time period, Fran also managed the Barrow Apartments, which were owned by her former employer, Pacific Architects and Engineers. At the time, they were the only apartments in town with flush toilets. Suddenly, the problems of the tenants of seventeen apartments became her problems.

Today much of Barrow is on the Utilidor. Those households that are not on the Utilidor still have water delivered, storing it in everything from large, insulated storage tanks to big plastic garbage cans. Sewage is dealt with by the "honey bucket" method, but regularly scheduled pickups make it more convenient.

In 1975, these basic needs were the impetus for Fran to

create two more companies, Iñupiat Water and the Elephant Pot Sewage Hauling Company. It was at this time that Fran's oldest son Mike moved from Auburn to Barrow.

"He drove the water truck for a while, and then I fired him. When five or six o'clock came, he'd say, 'I'm done.' I'd say, 'We ain't done,' but he was. Then I'd take the truck and make the rest of the deliveries. So I fired him, told him to go get a job someplace else.

"He went to work for a while as a carpenter's helper. Then he wrote me a really nice card that said, 'Mom, I really admire what you do, I'd really like to be like you and can I have my job back?' So I gave him his job back for about three weeks and then I fired him again! On his last check, I put, 'Bonus—$100.' He asked me what the bonus was for, and I told him it was so he wouldn't ask me for his job back!

"He started driving a sewage truck for the Borough. But when he first came up here, I told him about when I was working in the oil fields. So he said, 'Oh man, Mom. Get me a job working in the oil fields. The guys back home won't believe it when they see I'm working in the oil fields.'

"I told one of the foremen that I had a son up here who was six foot three and weighed two hundred fifty pounds who wanted a job. The foreman said good, he'd make him a roustabout, like I was.

"Mike's a big guy. When he played baseball, he always had the most stolen bases. The second baseman would see him coming and just get out of the way.

"But my son had never been exposed to anything like a drilling rig before. There's some big machinery on a rig, drills going so loud you can't hear yourself think. Pipe is going everywhere, chains swinging around—when that chain comes around, if it hits you it can cut you in half. You've got to be alert at all times on a drilling site.

"I took a picture of him the first day before he left for the job, in his hard hat and all his clothes—'On my way to the oil fields.' I had bought him $400 worth of clothes and boots, and he came home the first day and said, 'I quit.' I said, 'No, you ain't quittin'. I got you that job, you've got to stick with it.' He was making $240 a day, but the equipment scared him. The worst thing was, the first day he got there, they said, 'Bet you're one hell of a worker, your mom sure is a good worker.' He couldn't live up to that.

"After the second day he said, 'I'm through. I don't even care if they pay me. I just want to get out of there.'"

CHAPTER 9
Pepe's—Opening Soon

In 1975, Fran tried to interest McDonald's in a franchise in Barrow. She drew sample ads showing a dog team going through the famous Golden Arches at the top of a globe of the world. The letter went to the corporate headquarters in Oak Brook, Illinois. They contacted the Anchorage office who, impressed with the ads, told Fran that if she ever wanted a job at McDonald's, they could use a PR person like her.

But McDonald's was not interested in a franchise in the frozen North.

"They said it was a great idea, but they didn't go to places with less than 50,000 people," Fran said.

Given her financial situation at the time, it was probably just as well. "A franchise at that time—1975—would cost $125,000," she said. "Here I was, bouncing checks for $50.

"I started working on Pepe's in 1976, when I bought a

house in Barrow. I paid $26,000 for it, but the house was a mess. The windows were all boarded up, the doors were all broken, there were no steps, there were just boxes to climb up. The furnace didn't work. Sam, the guy I bought it from, had a son who didn't want to believe that I had bought that house. So Joe stayed there at night while I stayed at another shack that I had bought."

Son Mike said, "Actually, the first Pepe's opened in my house. My wife Cindy and I found a house to buy, and Fran had found another house, one that was closer to the school. That one was only one-story, fourteen-by-twenty-eight feet, and had burned down three times. She was going to put the restaurant in there."

"But I found this other house, a bigger place, right across the street from the post office. And she said 'Tell you what—let's trade houses.' I kind of said, 'Well, gee, I don't know…' and she said, 'We're trading houses.' So I got the little shack that burned down three times, and she opened up Pepe's.

"The house we ended up with was so cold," he said. "One Valentine's Day I got Cindy some dachshund puppies, and they peed on the floor and it froze."

It turned out that Fran wasn't the only one who saw the potential in the property.

"About six months after I bought it, GTE (the telephone company) came along and said they wanted to buy that corner lot because that's a nice lot," Fran said. "They offered me $60,000, but I said no. Everybody said I was stupid, because I could double my money right then and I hadn't done a thing. But I said money is not my goal. I said I was going to open a Mexican restaurant and that's what I'm going to do. My goal comes first, I don't care what GTE has in mind.

"Then they came back with a counter offer of $68,000. Again, everyone said I was stupid, but I didn't care.

"But the restaurant took a long time, because I took my proposals to eleven different banks in Alaska and they all turned me down. Then I went to the Department of Commerce in Juneau, and they turned me down, too. (The Department of Commerce made loans to small businesses that were directly concerned with aspects of tourism, such as guided fishing trips. Apparently their criteria did not include arctic Mexican restaurants.)

"The first bank I went to was the First National Bank of Anchorage. When I left Barrow, I was carrying a piece of two-by-four about eight by eleven inches. It was perfectly to scale with the building, and on it I had drawn how I was going to do the restaurant. I got the idea just overnight, so I grabbed that two-by-four and jumped on a plane.

"The banker said, 'Gee, I'd really like to help you because I like your story and I believe everything you're saying and I don't even know you. But it's very difficult for me to take this two-by-four and face the board and tell them I want to loan this lady $40,000, and this is what the restaurant will look like. Anything but a Mexican restaurant.'

"At that same time I was already in hock to the tune of $53,000 for a ten-plex I was in the process of building. I'm the kind of person, I go ahead and start things and then try to find the money. I'd already put the pilings in and the glue-lam beams, which cost me a fortune, they were about $4,000 each, but I was happy 'cause I just love construction. So I presented him with this ten-plex idea, and this was Package Number Two.

"He said, 'I can't give you $53,000. What will it take to keep you out of jail?' I said, 'How about half?' and he said, 'I'll give you $18,000, and you'll pay me back in ninety days,' and he just had me sign a note. He didn't take a credit report or know anything about me except what I told him.

"So I went back to work on the Pepe's idea, and started remodeling that old house, but nobody else gave me no money, so I started cleaning toilets to get some money together fast. I worked as a chambermaid at the Barrow Apartments, which I was managing. I cleaned the apartments the FAA had for $7.50 an hour. Scrubbed the floors and vacuumed and made the beds, cleaned the bathrooms. And I put all that money toward Pepe's.

"And then I cleaned what they call a 'humus toilet,' which was horrible. Horrible. They're no longer in Barrow. I charged $90 each to clean them, and one time I took Joe with me, and he threw up and would never go with me again.

"They were a big box, with a hole and a seat like a regular outhouse, so you sat up real high. In the box was the humus—dirt—and a paddle, so when you went potty you turned the paddle and it mixed it up. But when you clean them you have to go in with a three-pound coffee can and dish it out. Then all the liquid goes down to a drawer at the bottom about two feet square by six inches deep. If the tenants had a lot of beer parties, that thing would fill up, and you'd open that drawer, but you couldn't move it because it was filled clear up to the top. So you had to try and empty it, and it smelled horrible. Then some people would have the guts to say, 'Keep that door closed, that stinks!'"

"It was the worst job, and it's funny I didn't get hepatitis, because I was in there with a coffee can, no rubber gloves or anything. I'd scoop it out and put it into a trash bag, and I had to watch that it didn't get too heavy. But those humus toilets—that was the dumbest thing the Borough ever did was to put those in the low income housing units. Then if the people would have parties on the weekend, they'd call me at midnight—'Our humus toilet is running over'—and I'd have to go out with my truck.

"So I did that for about six months, and I had about a hundred per week to do. I had Speedy Secretary and the water company at the same time. Sometimes I'd work all night long. I used all the money to remodel that old house.

"I got two carpenters from Fairbanks, two older guys. They worked from April to September, and got everything in order. All I had to do was lay the carpet, which I did myself. Then I had to order equipment, which came to about $15,000.

"Anyway, the carpenters were ready to leave, so I got their hours and wrote each of them a check. Then they said they were going on to Colorado, and could they have a cashier's check? Cashier's check means you have to have money in the bank. The checks I gave them were no good, but it was a weekend and I figured by the time they got to Fairbanks and cashed it, I'd have money in the bank.

"When I went down to the bank to see the bank manager, Wally Smith, I was thinking, boy I'm in trouble now, but maybe this guy will help me out. So I asked, 'Where's Wally?' and the cashier said, 'He's in Prudhoe for a week. Maybe I can help you.' I didn't think so, but I said, 'I need a cashier's check for $5,700.' She said, 'I can handle that. You want to pay for that, or do you want to debit your account?'" Fran leaned back in her seat as she told this, her face studiedly casual. "I said, 'Hmmmmm, I'll just debit my account.' So now I've got a cashier's check for $5,700.

"I knew the day of doom was coming soon. A week later, Wally came back and he called me up and said, 'Fran. I've got a cashier's check here for $5,700 and you don't have any money in the bank. What are you going to do about it?' I said, 'I don't know. I thought maybe you'd do something about it.' He said, 'Well, I guess I'll give you a loan,' and I said, 'Thank you.' And it went like that."

"I put a sign up outside the building in 1976 on a piece

of four-by-eight plywood, wrote on it with spray paint 'Pepe's—Opening Soon.' But we didn't open until October 1978, so that sign was up there for two years. And when I finally opened, the superintendent of schools sent me a bouquet of flowers and a note that said, 'To Pepe's Opening Soon—we thought that was the name of the place.' Some people who couldn't read too well thought it said 'puppies,' so I'd get these phone calls asking if the puppies were ready yet. Then some people called it 'peeps'—'When's Peeps gonna open?'

"Anyway, two days before we opened, my restaurant equipment arrived. I paid the equipment place in Seattle with two checks, one was about $6,000 and the other about $6,600. The first one bounced the first time, but I told him to try again and then it cleared.

"But the second one—I wasn't open yet, and I was spending all this money and not making anything. The equipment was at Wien Air and it was C.O.D., so I thought, I'll give them a check and by the time it gets to Seattle, I'll be open and I'll be able to cover it. So I gave them a check, and got the refrigeration equipment and stove and all. This was the night before we opened.

"We opened the next day, October 20, 1978. We didn't open that day until ten o'clock, and before ten I looked out the window, and I was half scared. I'd never been in the restaurant business before in my life. I looked out there and there were seventy-five people waiting to get inside a place that only seated forty. It was the first real restaurant in the whole town. So we were going just gangbusters all week. Each of my workers put in over a hundred hours that first week. We couldn't keep up."

Bob Green came to Barrow from San Luis Obispo, California, in August 1978. His family was in the restaurant business, so he'd had a bit of experience.

"I was busing tables from the time I was twelve," he said. "I've been hanging around restaurants all my life."

His friend, Barry Smallwood, called him from Barrow and said that his boss was planning to open a Mexican restaurant.

"Bob didn't know much about geography in the Arctic," Barry said. "He was in shock for a week. I picked him up at the airport in the sewage truck, threw his suitcase on the hood and drove him to our little house on the tundra. It was an eight-by-twelve building with a four-by-eight master bedroom—that was mine—and a three-by-six qanitchaq. It was a nice little place. You could even stand up in it. And it was bought and paid for. I was squatting on the mayor's sister's property, but she lived in Seattle, so I didn't worry about that. But the shack was mine.

"I later sold it to a guy who couldn't decide whether to turn it into a tool shed or a bathroom. Then somebody stole it. The guy didn't see it for a year, and then one day he saw it floating on the ocean. Someone must have dragged it out on the ice and used it in a whaling camp. Bob's and my home sweet home."

Bob was hired to be a cook, but found that he would

have some other jobs first.

"Fran had me laying carpet, moving booths, stuff I never thought I'd do," he said.

The day before opening day, they held an open house for the town's VIPs.

"The furnace went out," Fran said, "but they didn't leave. They sat right there with their parkas on and ate their dinner."

Bob remembered opening day: "It was wild. We went to work about two a.m. and we were grinding cheese and making enchiladas all night long. We opened the next morning, and there were lines all the way down the street. I think all of us were scared. We opened the doors and it was just BAM! From that moment on it was a full-tilt boogie. That first week we put in fourteen- and twenty-hour days. And it really never let up. Needless to say, this was a little unusual for me and my kick-back California lifestyle."

Barry remembered, "About seven-thirty that evening we ran out of food. I said what are we going to do, close? Fran said, 'Make more!' So we made more of everything. The refried beans were an hour and a half project and the meat takes time to cook, so while everything else was cooking we had time to grate cheese and chop tomatoes. By about nine o'clock we were back in business. The customers just sat there and waited. Darned if they were gonna leave. They wouldn't have sold their seat for a hundred bucks."

"We just had a little building," Fran said. "The whole

building was only twenty-by-forty feet, including the kitchen, two bathrooms, the storeroom and seating for forty. The kitchen was so small. The steam table was on one side and the refrigerated table was on the other, and the two cooks were booty-to-booty, and when one wanted to turn around the other had to go, too. I had one cook that was six foot seven, and the ceiling was too low, he always had to duck. He used to work in his bare feet to make himself a little shorter.

"Meanwhile the check for the refrigeration equipment bounced once, and I told him to run it through again. He had done that on the last one and it worked, so he figured he'd take a chance. But I still didn't have quite enough money to cover it. So they called the police department, and the police chief said, 'Fran, somebody in Seattle says they have a bad check. I told them they must be crazy.' I told him they weren't crazy, and to stall them just two more days. He said he'd just pretend he didn't get the message. A few days later, the check finally cleared.

"At that time, the charge for bouncing a check was $6, so I always say I got a $12,600 loan for $12, which is a pretty good interest rate.

"But at the time, I was scared. It's funny now, but it was not funny then. Kim Moller (the police chief) could have said, 'I hate to do this, Fran, but you better come and turn yourself in.' But he didn't."

Barrow Utilities and Electric Cooperative also became an unsuspecting investor in the restaurant.

Pepe's—Opening Soon

"I also used Barrow Utilities' money to open Pepe's," Fran said. "By the time I finally got the restaurant open in 1978, I owed them for months' worth of water. I owed them about $180,000. I kept making all kinds of excuses because I was using that money to build Pepe's. Finally, they put the clamps on me, they just said, 'No more,' so I had to give them some money."

The restaurant's first menu was a single two-sided page and it offered the same Mexican dishes that have remained favorites since opening day. But the prices have changed a bit. In 1978, the burrito plate was $5.75; in 1996, $15.75. The first menu already had the Pepe's mascot, designed by Fran.

"I'm not an artist, but I took the pieces and put them together and had an artist draw it the way I wanted it," she said. "I saw a little igloo with a donkey tied to it in a cartoon, so I took that idea and stuck a little Pepe's sign on it. Then I saw this kind of lettering on another restaurant, not called Pepe's, but the same kind of writing, so I did that. This little guy I got from a swimming pool ad. He was wearing a swimming suit and sun glasses, and he was pointing to the product. So I gave him a Mexican sombrero and an Eskimo parka and boots.

"When we opened Pepe's, I didn't have a truck, except for the water truck and the poo-poo truck—El Trucko de Caca. So when freight would come in, like the tortillas, or bread, I'd send Joe over in the poop truck and he'd haul it on the top of the tank, the roof, the hood—anywhere he could. The police stopped him one day and said he couldn't do that any more because he couldn't see where he was going; he had eight cases of bread piled up on the hood.

"So I bought me a sled, a little kid's sled, about six feet long. I would go and bring eight or nine cases of lettuce, tomatoes, milk, and haul it back. I looked like a Czechoslovakian peasant. I had the rope tied around my waist, my parka on, my hood up. And it's a slight upgrade (from the airport to the restaurant), and I was pulling a sled with maybe four hundred or five hundred pounds on it.

"Then Pepe's started to pick up, so I bought a bigger sled, about seven or eight feet long, and I painted on there 'Tate's Freight Line.' I could haul nine or ten cases on that. Everybody laughed at me because they thought I was going to go under anyway. 'Why don't you buy a truck?' Well, if I could afford one, I would.

"So I hauled freight on my sled, until one day in March or April, when I went to pick up ten cases of tortillas at the airport. Each case weighed about seventy-five pounds. I put half of them on my sled, tied the rope around me and started back from Wien Air.

"I was hauling them, and I was going around the corner, and it was banked really steep, and the sled tipped over and it broke and spilled the boxes everywhere. That was the end of 'Tate's Freight.' Then I bought a used three-wheeler and made a little cart on the back. I didn't have any money, I couldn't buy no pickup truck. It's funny now, but it wasn't funny then.

"We didn't have any freezer when we opened because I couldn't afford it. We opened in October, so we didn't really need one at the time. I built a porch with a railing on to the front of my house, and put sheets of plywood around it. We'd pile up the frozen stuff in there, and then the snow would blow in and pile up, and after a while, I didn't know what I had in there. It stayed frozen from October until April, when it started to thaw, and we finally bought a freezer. When we dug down in the snow and ice, there were things down there I didn't know I had! I had inventory down there! Chicken, prime rib, all frozen in.

"People don't want to struggle that much any more," she said. "They want to be president of the company, second day on the job."

CHAPTER 10
The Restaurant Biz

Doing anything in Barrow is never quite the same as doing it anywhere else. This is certainly true for the restaurant business. Fran has found that supply lines can be hard to maintain in the Arctic. Not long ago, a forklift operator ran the fork into stacked cases of eggs.

"I told him where to put the forklift—there's holes on a pallet where you can pick it up. He went to pick them up and I said, 'You dumb son of a bitch, you're going to hit the eggs!' He said, 'No, I won't.' So he went ahead and put the fork in.

"I told that guy, 'You just stuck that goddam fork right through my cases of eggs!' He said, 'No, I didn't,' and he pulled it out and there were the yolks just dripping off the forks. I said, 'Explain that one!'"

Another freight handler smashed eight cases of white bread flatter than a tortilla by stacking a shipment of generators on top of them.

"In the winter, whatever needs to come in warm—like produce—comes in frozen. When a honeydew melon or a tomato freezes, you can see through it, it's so translucent. And the lettuce is solid ice. The frozen meat, on the other hand, they'll let that sit inside someplace until it thaws.

"The summer is just as bad. When it gets warm, by the time the strawberries get here, they've got whiskers—mold. I take Polaroid pictures and send them back to the wholesaler. Last time I wrote a note, 'Do all strawberries come with whiskers, or do I have a choice?'

"Last winter they delivered an order of pop. I always tell them to call ahead so we can open the cargo door to the restaurant, because we can't leave the door standing open when it's twenty below. So they didn't call, and they didn't come, and finally I called and asked when our pop was coming. 'Oh, we delivered that a long time ago.' Well, the guy came without calling; the door wasn't open, so he just left the pallet on the ground. And when pop freezes, it explodes. I went out there, there was root beer, ginger ale, orange, everywhere. It was like the Fourth of July. So I told them, 'You owe me another sixty cases of pop.'

"A case of avocados costs $114. And we make all our guacamole fresh. It takes twelve avocados to make a dish about five inches square and two inches high. People gripe because an order of guacamole costs $3.50, but at six bucks an avocado, that's just the way it is. We tried the canned stuff just one time. It was horrible. I don't want that, I want fresh. We make the taco and tostado shells, too. We buy the raw tortillas and make them up here. We use about twelve hundred tortillas a day.

"If you order paper products air freight, you pay more for the freight than you do for the product. And now with the Haz Mat (hazardous materials) rules, bleach and whipping cream in aerosol cans have to be shipped Haz Mat. You know what that makes the price of a gallon of bleach? About $15.

"And you're way up here, so the suppliers send you any darn thing—what are you going to do, send it back? Any more, that's what I do, send it back 'freight collect.' Let them figure out what to do with it.

"Sometimes I ask myself, 'What am I doing here?' I guess I've just been dumb from the jump."

She found that Barrow customers sometimes have unusual expectations. In an interview in a restaurant magazine in 1985, Fran said: "Most of our customers have never seen the Lower 48. That makes restaurant life a little different up here. One day a customer came in and ordered a burrito plate. I brought him his salad and a beverage. Then I waited a few minutes before coming back with his meal. When I came back he was already up at the cash register paying his bill. I said, 'Johnny, aren't you going to stay for your dinner?' and he said, 'Didn't I have it?' He didn't know it included anything else."

The weather is always a major factor of Barrow life. One year, the catfish for a Mardi Gras party was stranded in

Fairbanks because planes couldn't land in Barrow. "We just struggled along," Fran said. "We already had the crayfish."

That winter also saw a cold spell where temperatures hit minus 50 with a wind chill of minus 100. Even Barrow residents didn't want to go outside.

"We probably got fifty taxi orders a day, every day," she said. "Hamburgers, sandwiches, Mexican dinners. Even steak and lobster on Friday, that's payday."

It can also be hard to find good help in the Arctic.

"Once I had a cook that got busted for drugs. A customer came in here, just dressed in ordinary clothes, and said that he was a Hewlett-Packard repair man. He sat at the same table, ate the same thing every day for about two weeks. That table, number three, looked right into the kitchen.

"I'm so dumb about drugs. Somebody would come in looking for my cook and I'd send them right back to the kitchen. I just thought my cook had a lot of friends. But this guy was watching the traffic going back to the kitchen. Sometimes somebody would come in, have a cup of coffee. They'd have a little paper sack with them, like they bought something from the store. Then they'd leave and forget the paper sack, and I'd toss it under the counter, thinking they'd be back after it. I never saw anyone take it, but the little sack under the counter would disappear. I don't know what was in it, drugs or money, but my cook must have picked it up.

"One day another fellow came in and headed back to

the kitchen. As soon as the repairman saw the guy, he jumped right up. The guy ran out the door with this other fellow right behind him. He dragged him back by the scruff of the neck and caught my cook as he was about to go out the door."

The Hewlett-Packard repairman, of course, was an undercover cop and Fran lost another cook.

"Another time I was the one who got busted, just for—just for being Fran Tate. At one time I had five people working for me from Bogota, Colombia. Three girls came up here one summer, just came to Barrow on a wild hair, and they all ended up working for me. One of them had a nephew in Argentina, and he had a friend, Rafael, and they wanted to come up, too. I always had trouble with them because they all wanted to be paid under the table, and I'd say, 'Man, I can't do that.' I can't run a business and say that I don't have any employees. Anyway, they all left before Christmas.

"One day in December I went to the post office on my three-wheeler to pick up the mail. There was a package in with the other mail, about the size of a picture frame, in a brown, corrugated envelope, and it said 'to Rafael.' I just picked it up with everything else, came back here to my office, sorted the rest of the mail and wrote on the package, 'No longer in Barrow.' I was going to open it, but it looked like it might be a picture of someone's family, and why should I bother to open it? I just stuck it in the outgoing mail slot.

"I went back out, got on my three-wheeler, and was headed for the Weather Bureau, when I heard a siren and there was a flashing light behind me. A week before this one of my tail lights had been out, so I pulled over, didn't even turn the engine off, just hollered, 'I fixed my tail light!' But the officer said on the loud speaker, 'Fran Tate, get off that three wheeler and shut it off.'

"This sounded serious. So I got off, and he said, 'I'm going to read you your rights, but you're under arrest for drugs.' I tried to tell him he had the wrong person, but I had to leave the three-wheeler and get in the car. Then I heard him saying over the radio, 'We just picked her up here in front of the Weather Bureau.' I was half in tears. I said, 'I don't know what it is, but whatever it is, I'm not involved.'

"They came in my office, and they said, 'Give us that package.' I still didn't know what they were talking about, so I said, 'What package?' They said, 'The package you picked up at the post office at 11:02 this morning.' They must have been following me around for quite a while to know I was at the post office at 11:02.

"I told them the only package was the one for a guy that didn't work here any more. They asked me if I opened it. Well, of course I didn't open it; my name's not Rafael.

"They told me later that in the corrugated slots of that cardboard envelope, there was cocaine with a street value of $40,000. Four or five guys came in, and I recognized them because they'd been sitting in the coffee shop for a week, having coffee. They'd followed that package from Bogota to Florida to Barrow."

Every small town has its grapevine, but Barrow residents have said that all you have to do is think something and it's all over town.

"All this was about eleven-thirty in the morning. About one or two o'clock I went over to the store to pick up some milk, and the first person I saw came up and asked, 'When did they let you out? I heard you got busted.' It was months before that died down and before people stopped thinking that I'd been busted for drugs. And then one of the cops said, 'See, I said all the time that Fran wouldn't do something like that.' I said, 'If you thought it all the time, why didn't you take me aside and ask? Instead of chasing me down the street—I saw that in the movies.' I never thought anything like that would happen to me. But it did.

"Then we had a dishwasher—he only lasted one or two weeks. He came to town broke. They used to come to town, go to the police station and say they didn't have any money, and the police would find them a job, and they could stay at the jail and earn their keep until they could get a real job and find a place to live.

"So I got this monkey with a crewcut washing dishes, but he was some kind of psychopath or something. He'd stand still, not washing any dishes, just staring, and the dishes would be piling up. Someone would say, 'Come on, start washing these dishes.' And he'd say, 'Yeah, I will.' This was before we had a dishwashing machine, so we had the two sinks—wash here, rinse here. So he'd stand and look at the dishes. Then suddenly he'd bend down and go like wildfire. He'd scrub those dishes just as fast as he could, then he'd throw up his arms and shout 'Ole!' Then he'd stop for another half hour and stare at the dishes. He'd scare the cooks half to death because he'd be real quiet and then suddenly—'Ole!'

"Then I had another fellow—I needed a cook and Job Service (in Anchorage) called and asked if I wanted to talk to him. He was part Native, and he was born in Barrow. So I asked him about the kind of cooking he'd done, and he said he'd done institutional cooking for a year and a half, cooking for three or four hundred people. In those days it was kind of hard to get cooks up here, so I took a chance and brought him up from Anchorage.

"The first day on the job, I gave him his uniform. I noticed that he was really impressed with it—'Wow! Nice white uniform.' And he'd stand in front of the mirror, adjusting his hat. But I started him off with the first order, hamburgers. He had about three orders, and it was three hamburgers and a cheeseburger. So he put one hamburger on. I said, 'You've got orders for four burgers all together, why don't you put all four on at the same time?' And he said, 'No, I just want to take care of this one first.' So he stood there—" Fran mimed a cook pressing a spatula on a hamburger, staring at it and suddenly grabbing her forehead. "Then he'd flip it over—she stared at the hamburger, suddenly grabbing her forehead again. "Then I told him to put the others on, let them cook, but he said, 'No, let me do it my way.' So I thought maybe he'd got a better system.

"I let the first day go, but I told the head cook to move this guy along a little faster, not just do things one at a time. The head cook started teaching him the Mexican dishes. One day an order came up for a cheese enchilada. He said, 'Fran. I forgot. What goes in a cheese enchilada?'

"I said, 'Cheese, I think.' 'Oh, yeah!' he said.

"Then he put up an order, and it didn't have the rice and beans on it. I said, 'Wait, it needs rice and frijoles.' He said, 'I forget what frijoles are.' But it said right on the menu 'beans,' it didn't even say 'frijoles.'

"Then the police told me that they were keeping an eye on him. I was sure keeping an eye on him, because he didn't cook too good. The police said he was known as a Peeping Tom, and they'd already had reports on him. And this guy smiled all the time, especially when there were girls around." To demonstrate, Fran pulled her lips back in a goofy, toothy smile.

"He'd be standing behind the kitchen door, waiting for the waitresses to come through. Finally I said, 'Tell me a little more about yourself. This institutional cooking—where exactly did you cook?'

Fran paused for effect. "A.P.I. (Alaska Psychiatric Institute, in Anchorage). I said, 'What the hell did you cook there?' He was a patient there, and he worked in the kitchen peeling potatoes! I said, 'Take that goddam uniform off right now, I'm putting you on a plane out of town.' I couldn't believe it.

"I called Job Service up and complained because that trip was costly to me. I paid his plane fare up here, and the guy ain't even a cook. Job Service said that he cooked at an institution and I said, 'Yeah, the one he was in! Sure, he cooked for four or five hundred—four or five hundred nuts just like him that can't cook a hamburger!'"

CHAPTER 11
Pepe's Two

The present Pepe's occupies three rooms that were once part of the Top of the World Hotel, Barrow's largest hotel, owned and managed by the Arctic Slope Regional Corporation.

After the hotel's construction in 1974, they experimented with having a bar in what is now the Fiesta Room. Fran still lived out at "the camp" at NARL and worked in the hotel as a cocktail waitress in the evenings.

The bar opened 3 p.m. and if you weren't there promptly, you couldn't get a seat. According to Elise Patkotak, a New Jersey woman who took a nursing job in Barrow in 1972 and never left, by 5 p.m. it was impossible to get in the place.

"If you'd go in after work, about five or six o'clock," she said, "the place would be wall-to-wall people, and all you could see was Fran's hand up in the air above the crowd. How she maneuvered through that crowd serving drinks I'll never know. I think I went in there twice. I couldn't stand to be in the room. I don't know how she did it every day. The bouncer was supposed to count how many people were in there, and there was always a line of people waiting for someone to leave so they could get in.

"The bar was open less than a year, but the rumor was that during that time, it sustained fifteen years' worth of damage." The bar opened in October 1974 and closed March 1975.

"In the Top of the World restaurant (in what is now the El Toro room in Pepe's) I would make about $5 in tips," Fran said. "One party had a bill that was over $100 and they left me $1 tip. Then the same people went over to the bar and ordered a round of drinks for $20 and left me a $10 tip.

"People up here didn't really know how to drink," she said. "At first everyone drank beer. Then someone would order a mixed drink, and then everyone would order the same thing.

"One night there were two women sitting together at one table, and a bunch of guys at another. One of the guys wanted to buy one of the women a drink and asked what she was having. It was a double Chivas Regal. Seven dollars it cost. I served her the drink and then went to him to collect, and he couldn't believe that it cost so much. Then the woman turned around and yelled, 'You son of a bitch, if you're too cheap to pay for my drink, I'll pay for it myself.'

"There was a fight in that place every night. About once a week someone would go through that window where the piano is now.

"Nobody understood 'last call.' At twenty minutes before eleven the bartender quit serving, but the customers wanted to keep on ordering. Then everybody got smart and when I said 'last call,' the guy that was drinking beer would order six beers. Or they'd order double shots, order four double shot Bloody Marys. Then they'd only have twenty minutes to drink them all. By the end of the evening, some of them would be under the table. The booths had those Naugahyde covers, and they'd just slip down."

The bar closed after a number of drunken people froze to death. The room was converted to a second dining room for the Top of the World restaurant, which continued to suffer from poor management.

In 1980, a restaurant review in *Alaska Today* magazine was not encouraging.

"The salads are quite bad, with an emphasis on iceberg lettuce interspersed with iceberg lettuce," it said. "Seafood items are canned, salty and unappealing." The magazine did note that the menu changed completely every time there was a new cook, which was about every other month.

The same article called Pepe's the "toast of the town" and praised their use of fresh ingredients. "Considering air freight prices," it said, "getting fresh vegetables anywhere in Barrow is almost a miracle."

Later that year, ASRC decided they'd had enough of the restaurant business.

"Their help always came over to eat at Pepe's," Fran said, "and one day ASRC called me and asked if I'd take over the management. Well, taking over a restaurant that has a bad reputation is like putting a tuxedo on a drunk. You've still got a drunk. And I'd heard so many bad things about the place. So I told them that I'd like to take over the whole place and pay them rent.

"I was just getting ready to add on at the old Pepe's. After a year and a half, we needed more room.

"But ASRC said they'd have to have a board meeting about it. Three days later, on May 12, they said yes.

"That night I stayed up all night. I came down here, looked at this place and said, 'Oh God, I don't know anything about cooking and I have now got a restaurant that is three times the size of what I had.' As I walked through the building, it felt like I was walking for blocks. I didn't know if I could handle it."

She and Bob sat in the empty restaurant, asking themselves if they could pull it off. Finally, they shook hands and said that they'd try.

"I decided to remodel first thing because it was ugly, all dark paneling," Fran said. "The first couple days, I tore all that paneling off myself, working around the clock. I wanted to open on June 1, so I only had eighteen days. I put an ad in the Fairbanks paper for a carpenter and got two guys to come up. I have a friend who's an interior decorator in Anchorage, and she helped me pick out tile and bamboo for the ceiling. I had the ideas, but I didn't know where to get the stuff. I went to a junkyard in Anchorage one night. They were closed so I climbed over the fence because I wanted to get as much done as I could. I found

111

all the candelabra that's in the restaurant. I just set them aside and went back the next day and bought them. They were made in Germany and used to be green but I painted them black.

"Then I ran down to Tijuana real quick and got Mexican hats, tablecloths, paper flowers. I spent about $10,000 in eighteen days, outfitting the restaurant.

"We closed up the old Pepe's on May 31 at ten o'clock at night, and at six o'clock the next morning we opened over here. It was really funny, because we had never served breakfast before. We didn't know where the eggs were, the bacon, or the frying pan, because we hauled it all over at night. We were used to the Mexican stuff, that was the same routine, but the breakfast was all new.

"We opened in there on June 1. Then we took another sixty days and totally re-did the coffee shop. We used the same booths that were over at the old Pepe's. We opened the coffee shop on August 1, and El Toro on October 1, so every sixty days we'd open a new section.

"Once the restaurant was open, the carpenters couldn't work during the day, so we were working around the clock. Once I was eating about two o'clock in the morning, and I was so tired from working all day long and supervising the carpenters all night. I was eating mashed potatoes and butter and I fell asleep and my face fell into the mashed potatoes and butter.

"At least it wasn't gravy."

Pepe's Two

Chapter 12
Joe the Waterman

It's a blustery afternoon in mid-May, and Joe the Waterman is making his rounds in his enormous green water truck. Like many vehicles in Barrow, it has had a rough life and it looks it. The truck is missing both of its bumpers, but the front of the vehicle has a tire chained to its grille. The door on the passenger's side no longer opens, and the space where a passenger might have sat once upon a time is piled with cardboard boxes, tools, a grimy pair of binoculars, old plastic take-out containers, ancient newspapers, and spare gloves. The truck's dashboard, coated with several alternating layers of grease and grit, looks like it's made of some furry faux animal material. A series of jagged holes punched in the dashboard hold masses of keys, plastic cartoon figurines, and a giant wind-up alarm clock. Flying gravel has put a dozen round pock marks in the windshield, and the cracks that radiate from each of them crawl in a network that covers most of the glass. The bare metal gas pedal is encrusted with mud. A 125-foot muddy blue hose is draped on brackets at the back of the truck.

On his belt, Joe carries a radio phone that rings about every ten minutes. Each time he answers, "Iñupiat Water." Most of the customers simply say, "I need water," without bothering to identify themselves. Joe always answers, "I'll be there in a bit." He knows them all.

Joe is wearing his standard uniform—white plastic bunny boots (probably so named because they make the wearer's feet look like Bugs Bunny's), tattered orange plastic gloves, jeans, and a filthy T-shirt. Some cartoon drawings of walrus and whales and the word "Ipiqsi" are written by finger in the dust and mud that coat the truck.

"That's Iñupiaq for 'dirty T-shirt,'" Joe explains seriously. He pulls into a driveway that looks more like a mud lake. He uncoils the hose, running it down the driveway and through the mud, over the porch, through the front door and into the water tank. This house has an older, makeshift water system. The customer stands on a wooden box, watches the water level rising in the tank and hollers when it's full. Newer houses are built with a hose connector jutting out from the side of the house. For these, Joe removes the hose nozzle and adds an attachment that allows the hose to hook up, and the water is pumped directly into the tank. These uptown models have an overflow valve that shoots a stream of water out just above the incoming pipe to show when the tank is full. But if there's no other way to get the water in, Joe hauls the muddy hose through the house to the tank or whatever other arrangement the household has made to hold its water.

At the next stop, a chubby toddler in his mother's arms watches Joe as he fills first the tank and then a large plastic garbage can standing beside the washing machine.

"Joe-Joe truck?" the boy asks his mother.

"Yes, that's Joe-Joe's truck," she answers, explaining, "It's always a big day when Joe-Joe comes with the big truck."

Joe's mother Fran began the water business in 1977.

"I started the water company because the guy who was delivering water to Barrow Apartments delivered it when he felt like it," she said. "At that time, Barrow Apartments was the only place in town that had flush toilets. We had seventeen apartments, and if seventeen apartments have toilets that you can't flush because there's no water, you have a mess.

"I told him, 'Listen, buddy. You let me run out of water one more time, I'm going to get a truck and be in the water business myself.' Of course, everybody thought that was funny, ha-ha, that I would get a water truck.

"But I had been in the fuel oil business with big tank trucks for gasoline and oil for eighteen years, so getting a water truck wasn't much different."

In November 1976, she located an old truck that was for sale. It needed some work, but Fran called a company in her home town of Auburn and made arrangements to have the tank cleaned and covered with urethane to keep the water from freezing—an important part of doing water business in the Arctic. An article in Auburn's newspaper, *The Globe News,* noted that a former Auburn resident had purchased a tank truck from a local company, and that the truck was destined for Barrow, Alaska, after being refitted with foam insulation around the tank. The truck also needed a new pump, so Fran designed a pumping system with a Neptune pump.

"A water pump is different from an oil pump, because it can rust from the inside. Also, it's colder than heck up here, so you need a pump that can stay lubricated with water coming through it, and a compartment in the back with a catalytic heater to keep the pump and motor from freezing.

"Every time you design a pump, there are always things that you can do better the next time. But I always used Neptune pumps and their meters. I put a meter on that first truck, but we had so many problems. We started out getting water from the lake, and dirt could come in and stop the pumps. One little grain of something could stop the whole damn thing. We had a filter system, and that caught a lot, but still little worms could go through and then get caught in there. And if the meter jammed, then you had to use a measured stick, open the tank, and put the stick in to see how many gallons you pumped out.

"On January 7, 1977, I drove that first truck off the plane in Barrow. Day One I had one customer—Barrow Apartments. Day Two, I had about four customers. By the end of the week, I had about fifteen, and now we've got five hundred and forty-one. At one time we had nearly eight hundred customers, but since the Utilidor has gone in, more people have running water. And they thought I couldn't be in the water business."

Elise Patkotak remembered the early days of the water business.

"If there's one thing I remember about Fran and the water business," she said, "it was that when she first started, if her truck would break down, she'd get in a taxi and deliver five gallon buckets of water to get her customers through until she could make a delivery. This was back in the days before the Utilidor, when you either chopped ice or had someone deliver water."

Or you did without. Fran said, "I'd call Daniel Leavitt who had Tundra Taxi and we'd go around with those big white plastic buckets like we have in the restaurant. I gave them the water because I couldn't make the delivery. Just to keep up the service. Daniel used to say, 'I should take you for a partner, you're a smart lady.'"

In the scrapbooks of Barrow photos, Joe first appears in 1977, an extremely skinny young guy with long hair, sitting next to his grandmother, who made her first and only visit to Barrow at the same time. "Too gottam cold!" was Theresa's opinion of her daughter's adopted home.

There's a photo of Joe and his birthday cake taken in December 1977. The cake is decorated with the outline of the water truck with Joe's name written on the side, drawn in vanilla on the chocolate frosting. Perhaps it was an omen.

Fran remembered, "I did it (the water business) by myself until Joe came up in August of '77. But he first worked here in the Top of the World Hotel because I told him I thought I was going to open up a restaurant. He was a manager at Kentucky Fried Chicken when he was only nineteen, so I said he could run my restaurant. In the meantime, he worked here at the Top of the World Hotel restaurant and I ran the water business.

"At that time we had to go out to the lake (Freshwater Lake, about two miles from town) and drill for water. You had to drill a hole in the ice about twelve feet down, and if you weren't careful, the hole would freeze up behind the drill. I had a fourteen-foot auger, and we had to drive out on the lake, drill for about half an hour through the ice, put the hose in, pump out the water, and then come back to town to deliver it. It was more like delivering snow cones, it was that cold and slushy. If we could get two or three loads a day, we were doing really good.

"One winter day I told Joe, 'I need help.' He put on three pairs of sweatpants, two or three sweatshirts, a sweater, a Navy parka, boots, and he was freezing when he came back. He had a stocking cap pulled down over his head, he had a little moustache and that was just full of ice, and the snot running out of his nose was solid ice. He stood over the heater, shivering and saying, 'How much longer do I have to do this? I can't take much more of this.' I told him, not too long, just until I could find a driver.

"The funny part was he'd never driven a big truck in his life. We sat in the truck for two hours while I showed him everything—how to deliver and all—and then he was ready to take off. Well, this truck had microlock brakes, a little switch that you have to throw. He put it in gear, but the truck wasn't goin' nowhere. I looked out the window and said, 'He's still sitting there. Why isn't he leaving?' Finally I went over, threw the switch and off he went.

"And he had never driven a stick shift either, let alone a truck. Everything was totally new. He was about twenty-two years old, and it scared him to death. He was mad at me that day. I don't think he's forgiven me yet. Every so often he says, 'Where's that Mexican restaurant I'm supposed to run?'"

Joe remembered the first truck: "You had to start it by sticking a screwdriver in the ignition." One night in a blizzard he was driving the "lagoon highway"—a roadway (since washed away) that used to run along the beach. He could see the lights of a fast-moving ambulance headed toward him. Joe pulled over on the narrow road to give it more room, but he unfortunately was just at the spot where a drainage pipe passed under the road and into a big ditch.

"Suddenly, I was airborne," Joe said. "The truck rolled over, and I just hung on to the steering wheel. There was all kinds of tools and stuff in the cab, so that all got rearranged. I wasn't hurt, but the truck was upside down, so I went to get a front-end loader or something to get the truck turned up again."

Meanwhile, someone drove by, saw the truck, and told Fran that the water truck was turned over on the beach. Of course, she had seen the ambulance go by, so she called the hospital and asked if they'd just brought someone in. Yes, they had. How was he?—About to die from a drug overdose.

Fran went down to the beach to check on the truck—"her first priority," according to Joe—and found Joe and a few pieces of heavy equipment about to turn the truck right side up.

"What are you doing here?" she said. "You're supposed to be up at the hospital dying of a drug overdose."

Fran reassured Joe that he only had to drive the water truck until she could find another driver.

"I couldn't find a driver," she said, "and then spring came, and Joe started peeling off the layers. He went through the summer with just a T-shirt, and then fall came. He kept working in a T-shirt, didn't even put on a jacket, until somebody said, 'Bet you can't go much longer without a jacket.' So he hasn't put a jacket on since."

Joe can be seen on the streets of Barrow on the coldest days and in the worst weather delivering water in his T-shirt.

"His skin is like elephant hide," Fran said. "It's just thick. It's like he has no feeling. He wears gloves, because his hands get cold, but no coat. The whole thing started as a dare, and he just kept it up. And he's moving so fast, he doesn't notice the cold."

When Joe was young, Fran, believing that all children needed some music instruction, asked him what instrument he'd like to play, but none caught his interest. But when the Auburn School of Dance offered four free lessons to recruit new students, he signed up. After the first four lessons, he liked it. "It was something that he could excel at that his big brother couldn't do," Fran said.

He studied ballet, jazz, tap, and gymnastics. "He used to be known as 'Mr. Rhythm'—they'd put up three drums, he'd tap up them, tap down, do back flips, forward flips. I've got lots of pictures of him in his tuxedo.

"And of course the girls (in the dance class) all loved him, and some of them were a lot bigger than he was. Two sisters had legs like Clydesdales. They'd come running across the stage and jump into his arms, and he'd have to hold them up. I couldn't look sometimes, but he'd bend at the knees, and he made it every time."

Joe still shows a dancer's grace as he goes about his daily task, leaping from the truck, sprinting around the puddles in his enormous boots, coiling and uncoiling the bulky hose smoothly and seemingly effortlessly.

He's also a hard act to replace.

"Ten years ago, when he used to take vacations, I hauled the water while he was gone," Fran said. "People in this town couldn't believe it, but for three years straight I took Joe's place. If I hired another guy, then Joe came back to a mess because they didn't take care of the truck. So for three years, I took over for him while he was gone.

"One September he went to the State Fair in Palmer and he was gone for five days. It was one of those Septembers where it rained every day. I looked like an Alabama cotton picker, I was just black with mud.

"I pulled up to one house, and the guy said, 'As I live and breathe—now I've seen everything. Wait a minute, let me go get my camera.'

"I delivered water to one place where I had to drag the hose through the mud. Their water tank was way in the back of the house, and it was one of those places where you got to go this way, then that way, this way, that way. There was a bunch of guys playing cards in the back, and they said, 'Don't get the carpet dirty.' I said, 'You go out there and drag this hose in and don't get the carpet dirty!' How the hell am I supposed to get the hose in the house?

"When Joe came back and I picked him up at the airport, he looked at me and said, 'If I didn't recognize the truck, I wouldn't know who was driving.'"

Fran's other son, Mike, who was the first to do a stint as the water truck driver said, "I just couldn't work sixteen hours a day."

"But my brother is just as goofy as she is," Mike continued. "He's never had a paycheck. But if he wants to do something—like going to a concert in L.A.—the next thing you know, he's got tickets. One time she sent him out on a vacation, she sent him to Los Angeles, San Diego, and Las Vegas. And he called her from Las Vegas and said

'Get me out of here.' Fran said, 'What's the matter?' and he said, 'This place is nuts, there's women here chasing me—just get me out of here.' I told her, 'You would have gotten a call from me alright—Send more money!'"

In one of the scrapbooks is a handwritten note left for Joe in the early days of Iñupiat Water: "Lloyd is sleeping in the furnace rm. So you'll have to knock louder so he can hear it. If he can't, go wake him up. If he's not there, just go ahead and put water in the tank and put the receipt on the table. We trust you." There is also a thank you note from a couple for extra water delivered on their wedding day. A Christmas card from the same era notes that "You have given us such warm and incredible service, you deserve better friends than our family."

Joe stops in at Pepe's in the middle of the morning. The kitchen staff has set aside an order of eggs that were not done to a diner's taste, and Joe calmly picks them up off the plate and eats them as he relates the latest news from around town. His phone rings again.

"Iñupiat Water," he says. "I'll be there in a bit."

Photographs of the Barrow Apartments in the 1970s show a small shed attached to the main building. This was the "poo-poo shack" that housed the septic tank. Some of the photographs document a spring overflow, a cascade of brown icicles frozen down the side of the building.

"I started the Elephant Pot Sewage Company in November of '77 because the Borough only had a three hundred-gallon tank on the back of a truck, and they couldn't keep up," Fran said. "Everywhere you'd go, the septic tanks would be overflowing. The streets didn't smell good at all. I bought an old used Army truck from a place in Anchorage and named it 'Dumbo.' Bought a fifteen hundred-gallon tank and flew it up here. Then I was in the sewage business, and of course I couldn't find a driver for it either, so I drove the sewage truck until maybe January."

Allen Marquette remembered the two identical trucks with yellow foam insulation around the tanks. There were magnetic signs on the doors, one that said "Iñupiat Water" and the other, "Elephant Pot Sewage Haulers."

"The local joke was that if one of the trucks broke down, they just changed the signs," Marquette said.

The Elephant Pot Sewage Hauling Company was the first to offer honey buckets in "decorator colors." One customer said she was going to have one for the boys and one for the girls, since the boys always messed theirs up. One Christmas, Fran designed an ad that said, "Stuck for a gift for those who have everything? Buy them a new honey bucket." Over the years, the white, red, and blue models have been the best sellers.

"There were two other fellows who got into the water business," Fran said, "and they had all kinds of connections with the Borough, so they got all kinds of favors. They had all the Borough business, and the Borough gave them a truck and maintained it, and these guys got the profits. I don't play politics, so I just said, 'Keep it.'

"One of them happened to be delivering water to the

hotel the day I was hauling the poop out. And my truck was an old used one, but it was running! So I came in that day, and I remember it was colder than heck, and this guy said, 'Well! I see you've upgraded from water to sewage.' I just said, 'When you own your own trucks, it doesn't make much difference,' and they shut right up. And I went right on hauling the poop myself until I got a driver.

"Years later, one of them apologized for the way they acted, but the other guy—I haven't spoken to him since 1977. Right after I got into the water business he came to my apartment. He walked in and pointed his finger in my face as I was sitting on my sofa and said, 'Listen lady, I've got the water company in this town and you're not going to deliver water in your goddam truck.' Of course, I could have prosecuted him for threatening me, but I didn't know that then.

"Then one night after I'd been in business about two years, Joe had just put the truck away and the phone rang. It was about ten o'clock at night, in February, and it was colder than hell. It was this guy calling, and he said, 'Fran, you're not going to believe this, but my truck's broke down and we're out of water at the house, and we need water tonight.' I said, 'Is this some kind of a joke?' but he said that it wasn't a joke, that he could pay Joe for the water right then and to just send him over.

"So I called Joe and he said the same thing—'Is this a joke?' But he went back to the garage, got the truck, went to the house, and when he knocked on the door and said,

'You called for water?' this guy said, 'Are you kidding, you dumb bastard? I wouldn't buy water from you—' It was a joke! Not funny! He's lucky I wasn't at the end of that hose. I would have shot that house full of water. He was having a party, and one of the guests called us the next day and apologized for his behavior. They heard him making the phone call, but didn't think Joe would come, and then when he showed up, they felt terrible.

"But if we hadn't gone, it would have been, 'Well, I called for water and they didn't even come!'"

Joe heads the truck toward BUECI, the Barrow Utilities and Electrical Cooperative, for another load of water.

"This job is pretty easy when the weather's nice like this, in the thirties, not too much wind," he said. "Winter can get interesting.

"You have to go fast enough to keep the water from freezing in the hose. If you have any delays in getting into the house and getting the water flowing, this can happen. You got to keep moving fast enough."

But doesn't the water freeze as he drives from house to house?

"Not if you keep moving fast enough."

Once he fell on a slippery tile floor and broke his arm, which the hospital put in a cast. One month later, a customer gave him a hard time and he whacked the guy on the head and broke the cast. The hospital put on a heavier one, but that one was broken when the wind slammed the truck's door on his arm. With all the complications, he wore a cast for three months, delivering water the whole time.

"I could show you scars on my arms from where people have gone after me," he said, "not because of me, but because they're drinking and they're mad and I happen to walk in.

"I could probably get half the people in town in trouble, knowing what they've got that they're not supposed to have, or who they're with where they're not supposed to be. But—it's not my business.

"Maybe I'll just do this until I'm eighty and then retire. If I live to be eighty-five, I'll still have a little time to go to the State Fair and stuff."

His phone rings again.

"Iñupiat Water. I'll be there in a bit."

Chapter 13
Troubles

During the 1980s, Fran enjoyed national recognition on TV and in newspaper and magazines. It was also a decade of financial and emotional difficulty.

Fran's fast and loose cash flow manipulations were bound to catch up with her, and when they did, it nearly meant the end of Pepe's North of the Border. In 1989, she found herself at the end of her financial rope and was forced to file for bankruptcy.

She was advised that only a CPA could straighten out her finances, but the situation was probably already worse than murky.

"I turned my paperwork over to them (the CPA), and they were charging me a couple thousand a month," she said. "And they would take out their fee first, and I got way behind in my taxes. The payroll taxes got way out of hand. I had a bunch of crooks cheating me up here. When

I was building the Burger Barn, I had five Mexican brothers that took me for $92,000. Two of them would show up for work, and they would punch in all the other guys, even though they were home sleeping.

"The IRS got on me so bad that every time I had a $10,000 check coming from the Borough for water, the IRS would levy it. Meanwhile, I'd made a promise to someone else to pay them using that money, but the IRS would levy it. Since I said I'd pay the next person, they would make a promise to someone else, then because I didn't pay, they couldn't pay—it got so bad that I wouldn't put any money in the bank at all. I walked around with $20,000 or $30,000 in cash on me and made payroll by paying everyone in cash. Then the IRS went right to the Borough and levied the check from them. I had to survive—I was willing to give them part of it, but they took it all.

"I'd pay for everything with cash or buy money orders. The banker would laugh because I'd stand over in the bank and write a stack of money orders." (The bank at that time was in a building that looked more like a small house. After the modern National Bank of Alaska building was erected on the other side of the street, the other building was converted to a video rental store named, appropriately enough, The Video Bank.) "I didn't put any money in the bank for probably eight or nine months.

"So my banker in Anchorage, at the United Bank of Alaska—which also filed Chapter Eleven, after me—called me up and told me to come down and file for bankruptcy. He took me to an attorney who wanted $10,000 up front. I didn't have it, but I had another water check coming from the Borough. So he levied the check, and held it in escrow.

"Well, while this was being filed, for about six months that IRS guy would call me three times a week in the late afternoon—it must have been just before he went home from work. And he would say, 'I'm going to get all of that money if I have to step on your neck to do it.' Nice guy. Or he'd say, 'I'm going to come up and chain your door shut.' I told ASRC that, and they said if he chained the door shut, they'd come over with a welding torch and cut the chain."

About the same time, there was a change in tax rules that affected business owners, and Barrow's Rotary Club invited a speaker from the IRS to explain the changes. Their weekly meeting was held then (as it is now) at Pepe's. The Rotary Club specifically requested that Fran's tormentor not be sent.

"They said not to send this guy, that they didn't want him," Fran said. "Well, here he came up anyway, and he was just about to walk in the door when the president asked him his name. When the Rotary found out who he was, they told him they didn't want him, that they'd just have a meeting without a speaker. That's how well-liked he was." And how solidly the Barrow community could stand behind one of its members.

TROUBLES

"If I can't make money, I can't pay anybody," she said. "The IRS didn't seem to understand that. It was a tough experience, but I learned a lot and now everybody's paid off. March 1, 1995, I was free and clear. I only had thirty-seven creditors on the list, usually a bankruptcy has over a hundred. It was a six-year plan to pay everybody off, and they got eighty percent. Usually the creditors get thirty percent. I said I wanted to pay them off in full, but the judge said that I couldn't do that, because they would think that I could have done it in the first place.

"When I was in court, the judge asked if I could manage these payments, because he didn't want to see me in there again. I said that if the CPA said I could do it, I'd do it because I didn't want to go through it again. Then he said, 'I've got to hand it to you—you've outlasted three of your banks already.' (After oil prices crashed in 1986, nine of Alaska's sixteen banks failed.) During the time I was filing for bankruptcy, all three of my banks went belly up before I did. And I pulled through."

Bankruptcy wasn't the only problem Fran faced.

In December 1980, a young Mexican named Chico Ramirez was hired at Pepe's as a temporary cook.

Elise Patkotak remembered when rumors first surfaced about a romance between Fran and Chico.

"Rumors were all over town that she and Chico were having an affair," she said. "A group of us Barrow women were having dinner at Pepe's one night. It was busy, and she and Chico were cleaning tables, and as they were working together you could almost see the sparks flying.

"Each time they would vanish back into the kitchen, we would look at each other and speculate. We decided that there could definitely be something there."

Finally, Fran stopped by their table to talk. She suddenly turned to Chico, who was working close by, and said something to the effect that "if you don't do a good job, you don't get to share my bed tonight."

"That killed the rumor right there," Patkotak said. "No more need for rumors."

Fran and Chico were married in 1981 in a wedding chapel in Las Vegas. She was 52, he was 26. In their wedding pictures, she wears a long white dress, a feathery stole around her shoulders, and a crown of roses and baby's breath. She looks half her age. Chico looks at her, but Fran looks at the camera, her expression a mixture of happiness and perhaps apprehension, a combination not unknown to newlyweds. When she and Chico returned to Barrow, they dressed up in their wedding clothes again and visited the Senior Center.

"That was a big hit with the elders," Leslie Bagne remembered. "Fran was so beautiful."

An article about Fran and her restaurant appeared in *Time* magazine on June 25, 1984. In it Fran said, "This is the best of my marriages."

Chico was quoted in the article as well: "Since I was a kid I have liked old persons. Actually, there's nothing better than old persons. They know how to be human beings.

So I talked to her two sons and they said, 'Hey, it's your life. If you like her, why not?' I have never been so happy since I came to the U.S. in 1974."

The difference in their ages was not lost on Fran. In the same article, she said, "Chico loves children. I had mine twenty-nine and thirty years ago. But I gave him three grandchildren. I made Chico a grandfather. Sometimes I think about Chico outliving me. I bought a four bedroom house in Anchorage. That's his security. After I'm gone, he can raise as many little Mexicans as he wants."

Fran appeared that same year on "The Tonight Show." Johnny Carson had a moment of surprise at the difference in their ages, and the audience gasped, but Carson quickly added, "And why not? If it were an older man and a younger woman, no one would question it." Fran described Chico's proposing to her on a drive in the water truck to Freshwater Lake, and she glowed with happiness.

"And this is a good way to keep a cook!" she added, laughing.

"He was a great worker," Fran said later. "And everyone at the restaurant was all for it. He was younger, but what the hell? I could keep up with him; he had a hard time keeping up with me.

"But about two weeks after we got married, he stopped coming to work. He'd stay home, play with the dog, and—I found out later—smoke marijuana with his friends. His only activity was the fire department. He loved the fire department; he was an EMT and did a great job as a volunteer fireman. But we don't have a fire every day. So the people at the restaurant resented it because they're working and I'm down there working and he's spending the profits."

Bob Green remembered, "They hit it off right away. She was really in love. He was a good worker, but he turned out to be a deadbeat. With Fran it's always business first, and he just was not a business-type guy, which was a shame, because he was really very good with the public."

The marriage ended four years later in 1985, but that wasn't the end of her troubles.

Barrow Public Safety Officer Harold Snowball remembered a Christmas season in the 1980s.

"Somebody told Immigration that there were several illegal immigrants coming up to Barrow to work," he said. "One night, the DINS guys came and said that they were going to Pepe's the next day."

Snowball reluctantly went along as a representative of the North Slope Borough's Department of Public Safety.

"Fran wasn't very happy, but she really kept her composure. She didn't lose her temper, even though we pretty much took her whole staff, around six or seven guys."

Fran remembered suddenly seeing DINS officers everywhere in the restaurant with their hands on their guns.

"Here goes my whole crew out, handcuffed together through the restaurant and out the door," she said. "It seems to me they could have handled it a better way."

In an article in the *Fairbanks Daily News Miner*, Fran

described Officer Snowball as having "a real sheepish look" on his face. Snowball said, "I knew Fran, and I was living in the community, and here were Outsiders coming in, harassing my neighbors. I think Fran forgave me, but it still comes up in conversation every now and then. She's had hard knocks, but she's gotten through them. She really puts her heart and soul into Barrow."

Losing most of her staff wasn't the end of it.

"Then the Immigration guys said, 'You've got to pay these guys what you owe them before we leave town.' They won't leave town when they've got money coming, and they want it in cash. I had to go to the bank and borrow money to meet payroll. The whole thing made headlines, and then the rumor was that Fran Tate hires illegal aliens because then she doesn't have to pay them.

"When the Mexican guys first came to town, the Native girls just went crazy over them. They'd call up the restaurant—'Can I talk to that guy that's cooking for you? He's Mexican, he's short, he's got a moustache and dark hair.' That described my entire goldang kitchen crew and the waiters! But they'd all pass the green cards around.

"One of the guys got married and I was invited to the wedding. I got there, and the minister said, 'Do you, Juan Ramirez take—' And I said, 'What happened to the name Gomez? He was Jose Gomez when he left the restaurant. He gets over here and he's got a different name!'

"Now Immigration's got a system. You get their green card and just punch in the number over the phone, and

137

they tell you right away if it's no good.

"There were five other guys living in one of my places, and one guy smoked marijuana in bed and the house caught on fire. Another guy that was sleeping there got burned by a piece of sheetrock that came off the ceiling, and when he got sent back to Mexico, he sued me. The lawsuit was filed, and he wanted a half a million dollars. I looked at the name, I can't remember what his real name was, but when he worked for me he was Ephraim Gonzales. I told my attorney that this guy never worked for me, all my documents said 'Ephraim Gonzales.' So they threw the case out."

Troubles

CHAPTER 14
Heeere's Franny!

The front page of *The Wall Street Journal* on February 7, 1984, carried the headline "Hot Stuff in the Arctic: Mexican Restaurant Is Far North Success." Reporter Ken Wells noted the "iceberg-sized steak burritos" being dished up by Pepe's eleven Mexican workers.

The article said: "The difficult part in bringing Mexican workers to Pepe's, Mrs. Tate says, was convincing her first Mexican cook and her first Mexican waiter that they could survive in Barrow, a place as dark and wintry as Mexico is sunny and warm."

The story continued: "'It took me a while to explain where Barrow was and what it was like,' Mrs. Tate says. 'But after I got my first two guys in here, I had no trouble getting others. Word got around that this was a pretty neat place to work.'"

"Jose Gomez, 25, a cook from Guadalajara, agrees,

though he says he spent three sleepless nights after accepting Mrs. Tate's job offer by telephone. 'I thought the restaurant would be like a big igloo,' Mr. Gomez said in halting English. 'I thought we would be walking around in big coats waiting on tables, like this.' He assumes an exaggerated crouch to show how you might serve a taco in an igloo."

The article also mentioned the raids by the Department of Immigration and Naturalization Service in recent years. "Wouldn't you know it?" Fran said. "It's always during the busy time just before Christmas."

The article ended with a quote from Fran. "There's a lot of money being thrown around carelessly up here,' Mrs. Tate says with a laugh. 'I decided I'd like to make some of it.'"

Thousands of people saw that article, including a woman who lived in entertainer Johnny Carson's neighborhood. One morning, as Carson was going to work, she ran out in the street and told him, "You ought to take a look at this." One of the staff people whose job it was to line up interesting personalities for The Tonight Show called Fran and arranged for her to be a guest on the show.

Her appearance on The Tonight Show on March 24, 1984, became a classic. It was included in The Best of Carson and mentioned in the book *Here's Johnny,* by Stephen Cox.

Cox said, "Everyone has shared my fantasy of stepping out from that curtain to shake Johnny's hand, sitting in the hot seat next to him, and making the crowd roar—even better, making Johnny convulse in laughter, pound his desk, or turn his head for fear his dentures will pop out as he busts a gut at my ad-libs." He called Carson's interviews with "civilians" (that is, non-professional guests) "some of the most charming moments in television." He reported that some guests have frozen upon meeting Carson for the first time, finding themselves under hot lights and in front of an audience that expects to be entertained.

Not Fran. From the moment she appeared from around the curtain, she was delightfully in control of the situation. Her appearance on the show was unusually long, as she enthusiastically described life in the Arctic while Carson leaned forward, chin in hand, throwing in an occasional "Really?"

The ever-generous Fran brought him some Barrow souvenirs. She presented him with an oosik (a 3-foot long bone from a walrus penis). Carson took it, examined it for a moment and said, "It's not a leg bone, is it?" Fran tactfully explained that "every male walrus has one." Carson, nonplussed, blurted, "Somewhere, there's one unhappy walrus!"

Fran also brought along some maktak, attractively arranged on a plate. Carson avoided tasting it, saying, "No thanks, I just had whale for lunch."

Cox reported: "Following her, actress Amy Irving was the guest. Carson reminded Irving that he heard she had bathed nude on the French Riviera on a special private platform. 'What were you doing there?' he asked the actress. 'I was waiting for some walrus with a million dollars to come by,' she quipped."

Fran eventually met the woman who had suggested her to Carson, as well as the woman's "flaky, phony writer boyfriend."

"He wined and dined me the night after the show," Fran said. "We went to a big, beautiful Moroccan dining club. There were belly dancers and sheiks all over the place. You sat on a pillow, and they put a big piece of bread, as big as a table, and a big bowl of something in front of you, and you grabbed a handful and just ate it. It was very authentic. And this guy talked to all the waiters as if he knew them personally.

"But when it came time to pay the bill, his American Express card was no good, and I had to pay the bill. Mr. Cool. He never did pay me back."

In spite of being stuck with the check, Fran gave him permission to develop a film about her and Pepe's North of the Border. In a letter to her, he wrote about "creating viability for you in Hollywood."

"He said that he was going to write a movie about me, and right after the Carson show he took a box of things that I had collected, articles and things from being on the show. After I finally told him to get lost, I had a heck of a time getting those things back."

Another writer saw her performance on The Tonight Show. Larry Rosen, a writer and producer for Columbia

HEEERE'S FRANNY

Pictures Television, thought that Fran was "a breath of air in the television world," and wanted to turn her life in Barrow into a sit-com.

By February 1985, and after considerable negotiations, the rights were sold to Columbia Pictures for a TV series. At the time, it seemed that all was "go" on the series, and Warner Brothers appeared to be interested in doing a movie.

In January 1986, Rosen and Larry Tucker, another executive producer with Columbia Pictures Television, began work on the pilot. According to a letter sent to Fran at that time, Columbia was "quite interested in developing a television pilot and series based upon Fran Tate's story."

Rosen came to Barrow in November 1986 and followed Fran around for a week, holding a tape recorder in front of her "twenty-four hours a day. No, twenty hours—I slept four."

"I had the best time in Barrow," Rosen said. "Fran took me everywhere, introduced me to everyone: leaders in the local government, dancers, a fireman who was longing for the green grass of Milwaukee, a gay man who was escaping the inhumanity of New York City—an amazing bunch of people.

"It was something like minus seventy, and I wanted to go out for a walk just to experience what it was like walking around in a temperature of minus seventy. Fran took me for a walk on the frozen ocean, and she was wearing a pair of clogs, jeans, and had her parka open. I was of course completely bundled up."

Back in Hollywood, Rosen and Tucker wrote the pilot and began to pitch it to the networks. The names of Shirley MacLaine, Elizabeth Montgomery, and Rita Moreno were tossed out as possibilities to play Fran.

"There was a lot of interest in playing the part," Rosen said. "Madeline Kahn loved it, but she had commitments to other projects. And of course no star is going to commit themselves to a story idea; they want to have something written down."

Rosen sent a copy of the script to Fran, who still has the bag it was shipped in, with the Columbia label attached. The script is very funny.

Not surprisingly, the story is set in a Mexican restaurant in Barrow. The opening scene is strikingly similar to the one that began the series "Northern Exposure," which debuted some five years later: A newcomer from Outside arrives in Alaska by plane. In this case, it is a young surfer who comes to visit her aging aunt, a restauranteur, and to put the touch on her for $4,000.

The surfer arrives in the restaurant to find Fran in a Carmen Miranda outfit leading a conga line of customers around the tables. The surfer, who is on the verge of hypothermia, staggers in and asks if they have soup, saying "I'd like a large bowl poured down my parka."

The restaurant serves as a meeting place for the cast of oddball characters. They are drawn in goofy sit-com style, but with a quirky genuineness that is perhaps attributable to the writer having actually visited Barrow. Joe the Waterman is there, pretty much true to life, as well as a fiery Mexican cook with amorous intentions on Fran, and a gay New York waiter with a pet penguin that he keeps in the restaurant's freezer—a false note that is funny but unnecessary. In Barrow, reality is weird enough.

Best of all is the very realistic portrayal of Fran herself. The TV Fran struggles against adversity, speaks her mind in no uncertain terms, and has a warm heart beneath a brusque exterior—just like the real model.

There is very campy scene in the pilot script in which Fran is dressed in a flapper outfit and the waiters are in vests and derby hats. When asked is anyone ever played the piano in the Fiesta Room, Fran noted, "That's a player piano. We used to have Roaring 20s lunches, and I'd wear my red flapper dress, and the waiters would wear vests and derby hats, and we'd play old songs on the player piano."

Who says television doesn't reflect reality?

Looking back, the show could probably have gotten the jump on the very successful "Northern Exposure," but at the time, no one was willing to take a chance.

"We never could get any of the networks to commit to the project," Rosen said. "They all loved it but they were nervous. They were nervous about the location. 'Who cares about Alaska?' they said. This was a few years before 'Northern Exposure,' remember. They were nervous about it being too bawdy. They were afraid that we would run out of material—'How many cold jokes and polar bear jokes can you do?'

"But throughout the whole thing, Fran was having the best time. All told, she collected something like $12,000 just in options, and all we were doing was talking at that point."

"If it happens, great," Fran said. "If not, I'll just do something more eccentric the next time."

But it must have seemed a bit unreal. Fran wrote in a letter at the time: "The facade of glitter and socializing Hollywood style is an unnatural environment for me, and all this 'fal-der-ah' about some Fran Tate is almost unreal!"

Columbia paid for the rights to renew the option several times, and the idea of a movie or a TV series based on Fran's life was kicked around Hollywood for several years. At one point, Fran went to Hollywood and met with people connected with the project.

"I couldn't take it, I just wanted to go back to Barrow," she said. "Their whole life is just phony. One night they had me in the limousine, and when you drive by in a limousine, everyone looks to see who you are. The driver was a real nice black guy named Reggie, and I said, 'Roll the window down, I don't want to have a window between you and me. Roll down that window so you can tell me where we are.' Then he said, 'Check out the cars on either side, they're looking at you.' I said, 'Yeah, they think I'm Phyllis Diller before her nose job.'

"It's hard for me to put on a facade and act. I can't do that, I act just as stupid as I do at a hot dog feed.

Heeere's Franny

Sometimes people like your honesty because they know so many people can be so fake.

"Life up here in Barrow is real," she said. "I don't have to worry about dressing right, putting on the make-up, and acting as if I were somebody. My comfort and main habitat is right here in Barrow, where I can run with my zany ideas, act crazy, and get away with it."

"The whole thing was worth it to me just to meet Fran," Rosen said. "She is one of the most indomitable women I have ever known or even read about. She believes very strongly in what she does and who she is and has completely and utterly dedicated herself to a way of life.

"I'm just sorry we were never able to convince the networks that it was the right time to do the show."

Chapter 15
Saving the Whales

In October 1988, in the middle of the Bush-Dukakis presidential campaign, the world suddenly noticed Barrow's existence when three hapless gray whales became stranded near the Point in early-forming ice. By the time they were "freed" three weeks later, their plight had attracted the attention of most of the media-served world and enlisted the aid of such diverse groups as Greenpeace, the U.S. government, the National Guard, the Soviet Merchant Marine, the oil companies, and the Barrow whaling captains and crews.

Whaling is probably the single most important element in the Iñupiaq culture. There is evidence that the people who inhabited the area that is now Barrow were whaling as early as 2,000 B.C., using the whales' meat, bones, oil, and skin for their survival.

A whaling captain was traditionally, and continues today to be, a very important man in the community. In fact, the

Iñupiaq word *umialiq* means both "leader" and "whaling captain." In addition to leading the hunt, the captain provides the equipment and provisions for his crew during whaling season.

Whaling crew members usually have some sort of family relationship to each other, and often sport matching jackets and baseball hats with the crew's name—"Koopak's Crew," for example. Each crew has its own flag. In 1995, 158 whaling captains registered with the Alaska Eskimo Whaling Commission, although all crews do not participate in every whaling season.

The number of whales that can be taken each year is established by the International Whaling Commission; it is usually about 20 "strikes" per year. By definition, a strike occurs when an animal is hit with a whaling instrument. Sometimes a whale is struck and unfortunately lost, but is still counted in the quota. (A lost whale sometimes later floats to the surface of the open water. Called a "stinker" for obvious reasons, it is retrieved, but only its blubber can be used.)

The yearly quota of strikes is divided among the whaling communities, with Barrow (being the largest) receiving a larger share.

The year's two whaling seasons correspond to the bowhead's migration. Much of daily life in Barrow is postponed from late April through May, the season for spring whaling. Special church services bless the whaling captains and crews and wish them a safe whaling season.

Spring whaling begins when the ice covering the ocean begins to break up and channels of open water, called "leads," appear. The location of the lead is indicated by a dark cloud low on the horizon, called "watersky" or "sea smoke."

Bowhead whales use these channels as they migrate to their summer feeding grounds in the Beaufort Sea, and spring whaling is done from camps set up on the edge of the lead nearest to land. This can still be as far as 16 miles from town, and the sea ice is extremely rough. Masses of ice up to several square miles in size shift continuously with the winds and current, and when these masses collide, huge pressure ridges are thrown up. Crews can spend weeks hand-cutting a trail through the pressure ridges with picks and axes. The ice continues to shift, and leads can open and close very quickly. Sometimes a lead will suddenly open between the whaling camp and land, and there is a rush to move everyone to safety. Then the laborious job of trail-building begins again.

The *umiaq,* a wooden frame boat covered with skins from the bearded seal, is used for spring whaling. A wooden or aluminum boat would never survive the trip over miles of jagged ice, but the umiaq is light, flexible, and moves quietly on the water.

One of the whaling captain's jobs is to hire a group of Iñupiat women elders who know how to make the boat cover, sewing the skins with braided caribou sinew. Five to seven skins are needed to cover one umiaq. The seams are sewn "double-blind" to ensure that no water can enter. Unless it receives very good care, the cover lasts for only one or two seasons, since the sharp sea ice will abrade even this tough skin.

After the whaling crew has hauled everything by snowmobile out to the lead and set up camp on the ice, crew members wait, playing cards, joking, talking, or sleeping in the white canvas tents. Someone is always watching the lead. When a passing whale comes up to breathe, everyone jumps into action.

The crew climbs into the umiaq, which has been sitting equipped and ready at the edge of the ice, and they launch it into the water. Experienced whaling captains have an almost uncanny ability to predict where a whale will resurface. The crew paddles into position just above the neck of the whale, about 20 feet behind its snout. When the whale resurfaces, one crew member throws the darting gun, a combination harpoon and gun. The harpoon is attached with a rope to a float, and a trigger launches a bomb from the darting gun. Another crew member fires a second bomb from the shoulder gun. The explosion of the bombs kills the whale, which floats to the surface and rolls to one side, exposing a flipper.

Before the days of CB radios, a runner carried a small version of the crew's flag back to town to indicate which crew had gotten a whale. Today, everyone who has a CB or VHF radio knows immediately of a strike, but the flag is still carried back, and the whaling captain's wife or other

TACOS ON THE TUNDRA

family member puts it up at the house.

As soon as the news spreads, everyone heads out over the ice to help with the butchering. Bowhead whales are generally from 25 to 55 feet in length, and can weigh up to 60 tons. The thick layer of blubber keeps the interior body temperature high, so it is essential that the meat be cut up and frozen immediately, or it will spoil.

The crowd pulls the whale up on the ice using block and tackle. It can take many hours to pull the whale out of the water and to butcher it, and no one sleeps until the job is completely finished. Fresh maktak is boiled and served to everyone. The big slabs of meat and maktak are loaded onto sleds and taken to town.

Once it gets to town, it must be distributed, packaged for storage, and put away. Many people have ice cellars dug in the permafrost in which meat will stay frozen all year.

The meat is divided in a carefully prescribed manner, certain pieces going to the captain and his crew members, and other portions for the rest of the crews who participated. Certain portions of the whale are saved for *Nalakatuq*, a June celebration of the end of whaling season, and for church-sponsored feasts at Thanksgiving and Christmas.

The work is still not over for the whaling captain, his wife, and his crew. They host a feast at their house the following day for the entire community, Native and non-Native, with a menu that includes fry bread ("Eskimo doughnuts"), stewed fruit, tea, and coffee as well as maktak, whale meat, and the heart, kidney, and tongue.

The fall whaling season takes place before the ocean has frozen, and modern outboard motor boats are used. The whale carcasses are hauled up on the beach with a front end loader or other piece of heavy equipment. In the rapidly shortening autumn days, the whales are often butchered under electric lights powered by a portable generator.

But the whales that the Iñupiat have hunted since before recorded history are bowhead whales. The three stranded, soon-to-be media darlings were another species—gray whales.

Gray whales are bottom-feeders, dining on snails and other crustaceans that live in the mud, causing Yankee whalers to nickname them "mud diggers." The 30-to 40-foot long whales, which can reach 40 tons in weight, were also called "devil fish" because of their aggressive response when attacked.

Whales are divided into two groups: toothed whales, like the killer whale, and baleen whales. Both the bowhead and the gray whale are baleen whales. Bowheads feed on zooplankton—small shrimp-like crustaceans that are strained through plates of baleen, a keratin-like material that hangs like a vertical window blind from either side of the whale's upper jaw. Zooplankton flourish near the pack ice in the long daylight hours of the arctic spring and summer. The bowhead swims through this rich organic soup with its cavernous mouth agape. It closes its mouth, expelling the water and trapping the plankton in the net of

Tacos on the Tundra

"hairs" on the inner side of each plate of baleen.

Although gray whales were hunted almost to extinction by commercial whalers (it is estimated that there were fewer than 100 of them at the turn of the century), their oil was neither abundant nor of very good quality, and their baleen was too short and brittle to be valuable.

Although both the bowhead and gray whales are baleen whales, they have very different life styles. The bowhead whale can swim underwater for up to half an hour without surfacing to breathe and travels easily in icy seas. The "bow" from which it takes its name is an arched portion of its head, with the peak of the arch at the blowhole. If the ice is not too thick, the bowhead can push it up and break it or breathe in the space below the ice.

Gray whales surface to breathe about every five minutes. They spend most of their time in shallow areas near shore and are not adapted for or used to travelling under ice. Normally, they are on their way to their winter feeding grounds on the Mexican and Californian coast by October.

During the summer of 1988, the pack ice in the Beaufort Sea had been unusually heavy. The village of Nuiqsut, east of Barrow, had donated its remaining allotment of strikes to the other whaling villages since ice blocking the Colville River prevented the village's whaling crews from reaching open water. Temperatures were averaging 11 degrees below normal, and in arctic Alaska, "normal" can be cold enough.

Roy Ahmaogak, out checking conditions beyond the

Point on his snowmobile, discovered the three gray whales, desperately surfacing to breathe in a steadily shrinking hole in the ice. The whales appeared to be young and were possibly not very bright, or at least not very experienced. These whales didn't have the sense to know when to get the heck out of town. Their being stranded was possibly not such an unusual event; one biologist remarked, "what's unusual is for people to see it." And these whales happened to be stranded 14 miles from the only TV station in a several hundred-mile radius.

Ahmaogak figured that the whales would probably die before morning. Sea water can form a skin of ice in a few hours in sub-zero weather, and the breathing hole in which the whales hovered was not very big.

Anything the least bit interesting is a subject for conversation in Barrow, so of course Ahmaogak mentioned the whales when he got back to town. The news reached a man who worked for the local cable TV company and who had some new video equipment that he wanted to try out. The footage that he got of the whales surfacing seemed pretty exciting, and he thought that maybe the TV station in Anchorage could use it. He made arrangements to do a satellite feed, and the whales made their debut on the Anchorage evening news.

In the world of electronic media, news feeds out in all directions and in another 24 hours, the whales were in everyone's living room. As soon as American viewers got a look at the enormous, snubby, barnacled snouts poking out of the ice to breathe, the race to save them was on.

"Barrow found itself in the vortex of a media cyclone," Stan Jones wrote in the *Anchorage Daily News*. Journalists from all over the United States, as well as England, Australia, and Japan descended on a community of 2,300 residents. The 40-room Top of the World Hotel was overflowing, with reporters sometimes sharing space three to a room and television crews setting up editing rooms in virtually every available space.

Next door to the hotel, the staff at Pepe's, wearing T-shirts that said "International Whale Rescue Support Staff," was serving up tacos and burritos as fast as they could be made.

"There were crowds of people in here every morning," Fran said. "The media people would bring about half their equipment in along with them, and then they'd table hop, start out at one table, see someone else they wanted to talk to and move across the room. And we were running around, moving so fast, we couldn't keep track of them. You'd get to a table with five breakfasts and there would be three guys there."

The providers of the news that America was waiting to read, hear, and see were working against a 4-hour time difference with the east coast. To meet their deadlines they had to make the 28-mile round trip out to the ice each day in the frigid early morning darkness. The reporters asked Fran to open up the restaurant at 4 a.m.—two hours earlier than usual—so they could at least eat breakfast and have some coffee before heading out on the ice.

It was CNN who set the schedule. Crews from other networks and stations came into the restaurant and asked if CNN was there. If Fran said that they'd left, everyone would clear out. If CNN lingered over their coffee, everyone else would sit down and eat, too.

Fran estimated that business was up 20 to 25 percent during the whale rescue. Talking to reporter from the *Fairbanks News-Miner,* Fran summed up the media: "They're bigger spenders because they have expense accounts."

In her capacity as Barrow's unofficial spokesperson, Fran found herself in demand for interviews with those who could not make the trip to Barrow themselves. A radio station from Melbourne, Australia, did a telephone interview with her about the "whiles." And in Fran's collection of miscellany pertaining to the whale rescue, there is an order ticket from Pepe's dated 10/20/88, 12:15 p.m. In Fran's large, looping handwriting is written, "Mr. Abrahms from NY Times re: common feeling about the whales. Busy!! Couldn't talk." Below that, written with another pen, is "Sent T-shirt, brochure, pen, pin."

Meanwhile, out on the ice, would-be rescuers faced the problem of getting the whales from their small and shrinking opening to the open water 4 or 5 miles away.

Using chain saws, whaling crew members began to cut a series of holes in the ice leading to the open water, and some reporters made much of the fact that the very people who hunted whales were now trying to save these three. What they were missing was the fact that the Iñupiat simply don't hunt gray whales for food. It was somewhat like expressing surprise that a deer hunter would take the trouble to save the life of a horse.

At first, the whales seemed reluctant to move from the safety of the hole they were in. Temperatures dropped, the wind shifted and gradually the ice closed in again. A Minnesota man arrived with a bubbling circulator device that he claimed could keep the water from freezing. Although the idea was met with skepticism, he and his machines were taken out on the ice for a trial. The idea worked as well in the Arctic as it had in Minnesota marinas, and soon the whales were enjoying a sort of jacuzzi, and the holes were remaining ice-free.

The journalists, many of whom arrived in Barrow under-dressed for the weather, were finding that this was not the easiest story to cover. For the most part, the action was out where the whales were, and the whales were some 14 miles north of town. The first few days, everyone just drove out to the edge of the hole in the ice, and a taxi cab run out there cost about $50. But the increasing traffic made ruts in the ice that made the route impassable for most vehicles. Snow machine owners found that a reporter would pay $150 to $200 for a long, bumpy, numbingly cold ride out to the whales.

Many made it out there any way they could; observers counted up to 100 journalists, scientists and just curious people out on the ice waiting for the whales.

North Slope Borough's Search and Rescue Department generously and innocently offered to take some of the first reporters out by helicopter, and soon found themselves commandeered by the media to be their private escort service. During the whale rescue, their pilots logged in over 50 hours of shuttle service. In one day, they made nineteen trips hauling journalists out to the ice. At that point, they just said "no."

"Our business is rescuing people," a Search and Rescue spokesman said.

The Iñupiat continued to labor with their chain saws, forming what *Life* magazine called a "breathing hole assembly line," cutting a line of living room-sized holes 50 feet apart in the direction of the open water, some 3 or 4 miles away. The North Slope Borough put the chain-saw wielders on the payroll and provided coffee and hundreds of donuts, produced early each morning by Fran's second restaurant, the Burger Barn.

But chain saws could not cut through the pressure ridge of ice 200 feet wide and 30 feet thick that separated the whales from open water. To solve that problem, high tech solutions were being orchestrated on high levels.

Newsweek reporter Roger Rosenblatt would later speculate that "a quasi-technological curiosity was aroused merely by wondering if the rescue could be achieved by human ingenuity." It seemed like everyone was willing to give it a shot.

Tacos on the Tundra

Veco Inc., an oil field service company, offered the use of its hoverbarge, an enormous platform built to transport heavy equipment over tundra or water by floating on a cushion of air supplied by two enormous fans. The 185-ton high-tech wonder had been mired in frozen mud at Prudhoe Bay for nearly five years, and was freed only by several days of Herculean labor. Veco spent $15,000 to charter a jet to deliver new turbochargers to get the barge going. The National Guard dispatched one of its Sikorsky Skycranes, the most powerful helicopter in the country, to help pull the beast along, but it became stuck in the harbor and had to be towed back to port, having travelled only 10 miles of the 230-mile trip to Barrow.

The helicopter returned to Barrow and was rigged with a 9,000 pound concrete and steel "ice smasher." The helicopter, dangling the "smasher," flew over the pressure ridge and let it crash down on the ice. After a few attempts that seemed to have little effect on the pressure ridge, the effort was abandoned as too dangerous.

Undaunted by the failure of its hoverbarge, Veco donated the use of its AST, or "Archimeadean Screw Tractor," a machine described by its own company as "odd-looking." It was an 85-foot long piece of equipment that rested on two long cylindrical stainless steel pontoons that ran the length of it. The pontoons had a raised ridge that spiraled around them and were propelled by screwblades. It could travel on land or water and could break up ice. The plan was to drive it over and through the pressure ridge, open-

SAVING THE WHALES

ing a passage to freedom for the whales.

One Saturday afternoon, the Barrow airport was closed to accomodate the Air National Guard C-5A that transported the enormous AST from Prudhoe Bay. It had to be disassembled to get it on even a plane that size, and mechanics then had trouble putting it back together. It never managed to be used in the effort to save the whales.

Back at Pepe's, the stranded reporters tried to keep themselves amused. One morning, two of them began taping in the coffee shop, stringing cable around and turning on their lights. One went to the counter to pay for his breakfast while the other one kept filming.

"Twenty-three dollars," Fran said.

"For a cup of coffee?" he shouted, pretending to be indignant.

Fran, never at a loss for a comeback, snapped, "That was *with* sugar."

That night, the segment aired on national TV. Viewers had no way of knowing that the bill was for much more than a cup of coffee, and the telephone calls began immediately.

"The first call came from a woman in Tennessee," Fran said. "She said they had been to Pepe's and they knew a cup of coffee didn't cost $23, and I ought to be ashamed of myself for taking advantage of those poor people who were up there to save the whales."

Fran complained to a network executive and a retraction was aired, but the damage had been done.

Tacos on the Tundra

Meanwhile, back on the ice and two weeks into the rescue effort, all the whales were weakening from swimming against the current to stay at the breathing holes. Two weeks after they were first discovered, the smallest and probably youngest whale, nicknamed "Bone" for the excessively worn condition of his snout, vanished under the ice. Biologists had noticed that its breathing was raspy, and they speculated that it might have pneumonia.

It appeared to observers that the other two whales had lingered because of Bone's weakened condition. With Bone gone, the two older whales began to move into the line of holes.

North Slope Borough Department of Wildlife Management biologist Craig George later said, "The whales had to teach us what they wanted. After a couple of days, they would move readily between the holes. The problem sometimes was to keep them out of the holes while we were working."

"The Eskimos were cutting more holes, and the whales were barely giving them enough time to move the ice away," Greenpeace's Cindy Lowry said in *Audobon* magazine. "I was cringing because sometimes the whales would come up into the next hole, just inches from the chainsaws."

There was still the problem of the pressure ridge. Scientists doubted that the whales would risk swimming such a long distance under the ice. There was also a good chance that the pressure ridge went all the way to the ocean floor. If they could not find a way to open a channel through the ridge, 85 Eskimos would have cut and moved 800 tons of sea ice for nothing.

After diplomatic negotiations between the Soviet and American governments, the Soviet Union dispatched two ships, the Arsenev and the icebreaker Admiral Makarov, from a polar drift-ice research station nearly 300 miles away. The Admiral Makarov finally broke through a pressure ridge 20 feet high and 100 feet wide, clearing a ice-free path.

On October 29, six days after Bone's death, the whales moved through the channel and into open water. By then nearly everyone was tired of the event, except possibly the town's taxi drivers.

The *Anchorage Daily News* later wrote: "For all the hundreds of thousands of dollars spent in modifying and bringing exotic equipment to Barrow for the rescue, in the end it was the Soviet ships and the muscle power and single-minded determination of the Eskimo whalers with their donated chainsaws that won the battle."

The cost of the rescue ran well over $1 million, and not everyone agreed that it was worth it, or that it should have been attempted at all. Craig Medred of the *Anchorage Daily News* wrote, "The cold harsh reality is that there is no reason to save these whales. All we are saving them from is the natural world of which they are a part."

But Suzan Nightingale of the same newspaper had a theory about the whales' attraction. "Sometimes, the world is too big and too impersonal and, yes, too messed up even to grasp; we are selective in our concerns out of self defense. We take on what we can because we can. It is emotional triage, pure and simple."

Then, as a headline in the *Detroit Free Press* put it, "With whales gone, Barrow returns to merely unusual." Reporters filed their last stories, hastily packed up their equipment, and fought each other for seats on the next plane out.

Greg Lefevre of CNN wrote a thank-you note to Fran for the extra hours the restaurant had stayed open and "for all the great meals!" Not every one was so kind. Tom Rose, covering the whale rescue for a Japanese TV network, later wrote a book titled *Freeing the Whales: How the Media Created the World's Greatest Non-event.* People in Barrow refer to it as the "whale-of-a-lie" book.

"He said in the book that we charged $23 for a greasy hamburger," Fran said. "Now when did we ever charge $23 for a hamburger? As a matter of fact, when they were here, it was right in the middle of Pepe's tenth anniversary, and Mexican dinners were $10.

"He (Rose) sat here in the restaurant and interviewed me for two hours. And we were busy at that time! And I gave him the names of everyone in town that he should contact, and then he turns around and writes something like that."

Fran wasn't the only one who was annoyed. Elise Patkotak wrote a review for *The Barrow Sun* and said of the book: "I don't know which is my favorite part. It could be where he describes going to the bathroom outside while simultaneously fending off dogs and polar bears. That sounds like fun. Or it could be when he claims we have wind chill factors of 174 degrees below zero. I think he has us confused with Mars."

"Why do people do this to us?" she wondered. "Isn't Barrow exotic enough without making up even more fantastic details?"

CHAPTER 16
Diabetes

Fran has never taken care of her health. She has always relied on her incredible stamina and energy to carry her through whatever outrageous demands she makes on her body. This stubborn refusal to accept her body's limitations nearly cost her life.

As a child, she seemed to thrive on the hard life on her family's small farm. But in the fourth grade, her German mother's health regimen of onion sandwiches and long underwear failed, and Fran suffered a bad case of bronchial pneumonia, accompanied by a raging fever. This was followed closely by the measles. At the end of it, she weighed 40 pounds.

"I can remember being a bag of bones," she said. "I looked like those kids from Somalia. I didn't even weigh as much as those sacks of chicken feed I was supposed to be lifting."

She enjoyed good health during the rest of her childhood and her early adult life, in spite of her always grueling schedule. The family doctor told her mother (who was worried that her child never wanted to sleep), "When she grows up, make sure she doesn't judge other people by her own capacity."

But in 1984, she had bunions "as big as ping pong balls," a condition that forced her to cut big holes in her tennis shoes and to wear Eskimo sealskin slippers for a year and a half.

"It was funny how I discovered I had bunions," she said. "I went to Anchorage to take care of things—dentist, attorney, Pap smear. I went to the gynecologist, who's an old-time, fatherly-type doctor, and he's got those cute pink crocheted things over the stirrups. So I'm up there with my feet in the stirrups, and it's not a comfortable feeling anyway, and right away he said, 'You've got to have an operation.' I said, 'On what?' He said, 'You've got bunions.' I said, 'Where the hell are you looking!?'"

The doctor didn't allow Fran the opportunity to escape; he sent her directly to the office of a nearby orthopedic surgeon, who in turn wanted to send her directly to the hospital. Fran pleaded for time "to get used to this idea," but two weeks later she was admitted to the hospital and the bunionectomies were performed.

"They (the nurses) told me to call when I needed to go to the bathroom, and they'd bring the bedpan," Fran said. "I thought, I ain't using no bedpan. So I swung my feet over the bed, and my feet just throbbed. There was a table next to the bed, so I hung on to that and swung myself down to the floor and just crawled on my knees and elbows to the bathroom. I was crawling back, in one of those cute hospital nighties that has everything hanging out, and just then the doctor came in. He said, 'I told you not to get up to go to the bathroom.' I said, 'I'm not up, I'm down here on the floor.'

"I had a cast on each foot," she said. "Each cast weighed fifteen pounds. One of them was so damn tight—my leg just throbbed. I said, 'You've got to take this thing off.' They gave me a pill—I threw the pill back at them. The nurse said she didn't have any authorization to do anything about it, and that when the doctor came in the next morning he could change it. Well, I had my purse with me, and in there I had a Swiss army knife. So I cut that sucker open. I'm a terrible patient.

"Then, when it came time to go home, they told me I had to have someone drive me. I had driven my own car in and had the operation all by myself. I didn't want to take a cab and leave my car there. They said, 'You can't drive, you've got two casts on your feet, and we don't know how woozy you are.' They made me call my son Mike, so I called him, but I told him, 'You don't have to come get me, but if anybody calls to check, tell them you're on your way.' Then I asked them if I could wait in the lobby, so they rolled me down in a wheelchair and left me sitting by the optical office, and I waited until the coast was clear. I had a pair of crutches, so I got out of the wheelchair and into my car and **I drove home!** I only had to work one pedal, either the gas or the brake, and my feet were heavy enough—I just laid it on there. Got home and crutched myself up to the house.

"I came back up to Barrow the next day. It was tourist season, so I worked with my crutches. I bet I got twenty letters that said, 'We had a great time in Barrow, and tell that waitress that was on crutches with two casts on her feet…' A lot of the senior citizens told me that they had one foot operated on but they never did the other one. My doctor told me he was going to do both at the same time because otherwise I'd never come back. It's so painful."

At the time, it was assumed that the bunions were caused by Fran's wearing high heels during many years working as a cocktail waitress and by being on her feet for such long hours during most of her life. No one mentioned diabetes.

A routine blood screen might have revealed the problem, but Fran has had a fear of needles since a childhood vaccination became infected.

"I've had thirty-three fillings and a root canal, all without Novocaine. Every time I go to the doctor and they ask, 'Are you allergic to anything?' I write, 'Yes, needles.'"

In 1986, a year of many difficulties for Fran, she developed trigger fingers.

"Your joints lock down," she said. "If I would grab on to a soup ladle, I couldn't let go. It doesn't hurt when they snap down, but when you try to straighten it out, it hurts like hell."

After an operation, she had casts on both hands. Of course, she went right back to work, balancing trays on the casts and using the ends of her protruding fingers. She even made a court appearance for bankruptcy with her hands in casts.

Another foot operation was performed when her toes began curling under, a condition called "hammer toes." Bones were removed from her toes, resulting in toes that are like little limp balloons.

"It's hard to walk barefoot—I have to walk like I've got diving flippers on," she said. "I have to lift my foot up a couple extra inches so I don't drag my toes on the ground." Still, there was no suspicion that there might be a more sinister underlying problem.

In 1988, a nurse from the hospital who was eating dinner at Pepe's first suspected that Fran might be diabetic.

"Everybody knows how wired-up I always am," Fran said. "But she asked me if I'd ever been tested for diabetes, and if I drank a lot of fluids. Well, I was drinking about twelve cans of Diet Pepsi every day. She said there was something about my eyes that made her think I might have high blood sugar. I didn't believe it—I felt great."

The nurse urged her to have a blood test, assuring the reluctant Fran—with her aversion to needles—that it would only be a prick of her finger.

Instead of the normal 90 to 120, the result was over 600.

"They told me I should be flat on the floor instead of up running around," Fran said. "They said I should be in the Guinness Book of World Records."

The diagnosis was adult-onset diabetes, brought on by stress. That year Fran's husband had left her and her troubles with the IRS had reached a point where she was forced to file for bankruptcy.

"I was so hyped up, I could have worked twenty-eight hours a day," she said. "My mind was turning constantly. It was during that time that I was walking around with from $15,000 to $30,000 in cash on me. I couldn't put it in the bank because the IRS would take it."

Dr. Milton J. Brothers, in his book *Diabetes: The New Approach,* writes: "It is not an uncommon experience for the onset of diabetes to coincide with an emotionally critical occurrence in the life of the patient; the emotional crisis is not the causative factor in the onset of diabetes; it is rather a stress factor that triggers the disorder."

Fran is what is known as a "brittle diabetic"—meaning her blood sugar levels are very hard to control, even with insulin.

"When the doctor first told me that I was diabetic, I was ready to jump out the window, just end it all right there," she said. "But he said, 'No, you can live with it. You can learn to control it.' Well, what I learned is it controls you. Every day's a new ball game. I can eat the same things, work and sleep the same amount, but one day my blood sugar's 400 and the next day it's 17."

But the old habits of overwork and neglecting her health were hard to break.

"I wasn't feeling good one Saturday," Fran said, "so I told everyone at the restaurant that I was going home and would be back at six o'clock. I took a can of juice with me. Just before six, I called and told them to bring me another can of juice, I was so thirsty. I started throwing up, just fluid. I had taken my insulin but what I didn't realize was that if you throw up, you also lose your insulin. Somebody brought the juice by, and I thought, 'I'll just drink this other can of juice.' But when I got back from the hospital, it was still sitting on the counter. I must have passed out about then, because I never got the can opened."

Fran was exhibiting signs of a diabetic coma—fatigue, excessive thirst, and nausea.

Without insulin to metabolize glucose, the body begins to burn fats. The by-products of fat metabolism cause acidosis, and the body's attempts to counteract this result in dehydration. The patient's blood pressure drops and the circulatory system collapses.

"Of course, I didn't go back to the restaurant, so about ten o'clock Joe-Joe stopped by to see how I was. I was laying on the floor, face down. He told everyone, she's really tired, just let her sleep." Fran is known for her ability to fall asleep under strange conditions, usually the result of continuing to work until she collapses. "He told Matt (the carpenter) to come by and check on me. So about nine-thirty the next morning he came in.

"I was still on the floor, only now my hands were all puffed up and white, and my dogs were sitting on top of me. He knew I was either dead or near dead. He called the paramedics, and they took me to the hospital."

Dr. Maria Freeman, a sophisticated young woman from New York City, had recently arrived in Barrow to begin the customary 2-year stint for which doctors contract. She was the doctor on call early Sunday morning a few weeks before Christmas when a comatose patient was brought by ambulance, accompanied by a large group of very concerned people.

It is not unusual for Barrow patients to be surrounded by relatives and friends, but this was quite a crowd. Although Dr. Freeman had not yet met Fran, she had heard of her, and another memory stirred in the back of her mind, a memory that was pushed aside as she turned to the huge task of keeping the comatose woman alive.

"I knew there was a history of diabetes, so the first thing I thought was that she might be hypoglycemic—that her glucose was too low," Dr. Freeman said. "We started to give glucose and did a quick check of her blood by finger stick. The little machine that we had in the ER said that it was high, which we thought was unusual, but we stopped the glucose while we waited for the lab results.

"When they came back, the glucose was astronomically high. She was hyperglycemic—too much glucose. The result was over 1800. Normal value is from 90 to 120. I'd never seen a blood glucose higher than 1000. When we saw that, we knew she was in a lot of trouble."

The next step was to push insulin, giving a large initial dose and starting an insulin drip.

Nurses and lab technicians drew blood constantly, monitoring blood gases and the basic chemistries of the body, elements that are drastically affected by such an extremely high glucose. In a case like Fran's, Dr. Freeman said, the survival rate is only about 50 percent.

Fran lay in a coma for 8 hours, completely unresponsive. The 14-bed hospital in Barrow provides health care for all 8,000 residents of the North Slope and treats thousands of outpatients each month, but—like most small, rural hospitals—it is limited in the extent of intensive care it can provide. Although Fran desperately needed a full-scale intensive care unit, she was too sick to transfer. The Barrow hospital staff converted a room to an intensive care area and constantly monitored her condition. Meanwhile, the restaurant staff paced the halls, crying.

It took 12 hours to bring the blood glucose under control. Fran was starting to come around, but still didn't know where she was or what had happened. Freeman tried to assess neurological deficit—something that is very difficult to do when the patient is in a coma. One side of Fran's body showed neurological damage, and there was a possibility that she'd had a stroke.

Thirty-six hours after going into the coma, her condition was judged stable enough for her to be medevaced.

Barrow's extreme isolation makes transferring emergency

patients even more challenging than it is in the rest of the world. With no road system, emergency cases are flown—weather permitting—to either Anchorage or Fairbanks by the North Slope Borough Search and Rescue Department.

After arriving at Providence Hospital in Anchorage, another 24 hours passed before Fran regained consciousness. A CAT scan was performed. The doctor telephoned Joe and told him that there was an 80 percent chance Fran had had a stroke and that she probably would be paralyzed or have brain damage.

"I told the doctor that if it was brain damage, up here in Barrow nobody would notice," Joe said.

He continued, "The nurses told me that when she woke up she was saying something, but they didn't understand what she was talking about. They said she was saying something about 'jazz below zero' and asking what are all these nurses doing here. I told them, if she's talking about 'Jazz Below Zero,' you don't need to check her any more. Just go on and send her home, she's going to be all right."

"They told me my eyes opened a couple hours before I could talk," Fran said. "I remember there was a nurse with a little name tag that said 'Gail.' They kept talking to me, and once she came over and asked how I was, and I said, 'Hi, Gail.' The next question was if I knew what day it was. They had a calendar hanging up, so I looked at it and said 'December 7.' Then they asked me what happened on December 7. Well, they had to ask an old lady that, a young person wouldn't know—Pearl Harbor. Then they said that I'd probably be okay."

Needless to say, Fran wasn't a model patient, dragging herself out of bed and into the bathroom, hauling her IV apparatus around the hospital with her. Shortly after Fran woke up, Leslie Bagne came to visit.

"She really scared a lot of people," Bagne said. "I went to the hospital not knowing what I would encounter. The news wasn't good; she was in intensive care and I was ready for the strong nurses to not let me in."

Bagne heard Fran before she saw her, a voice from the end of the hall demanding "when the hell am I getting out of here?"

"I thought she was still in a coma, and since I believe music is very healing, I brought some compact discs and a portable CD player and was planning to convince the nurses to play it in her room," Bagne said. "It was classical and baroque music, and it might have driven her out of her gourd. One way or another, I guess it would have gotten her out of her bed."

Fran's son Mike, who lives in Anchorage, rushed back to the hospital when he got word that she'd come out of the coma.

"We got to her room and Fran's on the edge of the bed and the poor nurse was there. Fran's yelling, 'Get the hell away from me, I gotta get out of this goddam place!' I told the nurse, 'She's gonna be okay. You guys better turn her loose or she'll be tearing the place up.' Sure enough, they let her go the next day," he said.

"I got out of the hospital and flew back to Barrow," Fran said. "I got in at seven o'clock that night and worked until two a.m. I had so much to catch up on."

"She's a very, very fortunate person," Dr. Freeman said later. "She came out of it with no neurological problems whatsoever. And she's very grateful to all the doctors and to Providence—and that's not only 'Providence' the hospital—that she's still alive. She sees it as a sign that she wasn't meant to die."

"Grateful" doesn't quite describe Fran's feeling about her survival. Fran cannot encounter Dr. Freeman in the restaurant or anywhere else in town without hugging and kissing her, demonstrations that both please and slightly embarrass the physician.

"She needs to realize that any physician here would have done the same thing," Dr. Freeman said. "I wish I could get that across to her." She probably never will, but the undying gratitude of Fran Tate is something worth having. Fran sends Dr. Freeman flowers on the anniversary of her "crisis," and never misses an opportunity to praise the hospital and the EMS workers in Barrow.

"Dr. Maria Freeman—I'll love that woman as long as I live."

After Fran was reported in stable condition in Providence Hospital, Dr. Freeman could then focus on the vague memory that had begun that Sunday morning when Fran first arrived in the emergency room. In one of Life's many cosmic coincidences, Fran may have been the reason that Maria Freeman, a black woman born in Wales and raised in New York City, made the decision to come to Barrow.

"It was a few years after I'd finished medical school, and I was living in New York," Freeman said. "I had the radio on in my apartment, and there was a program about Alaska. They talked about the coldest spot in Alaska—Barrow. They interviewed a woman who owned a restaurant in Barrow, and she talked about the life up here, and it was so intriguing. This was long before I even thought about coming to Alaska, I didn't even know where Barrow was on a map. But to think that all those years later, I would come to Barrow and that one morning this same woman would come into the ER, and that I would help save her life—it's incredible. She's been an influence on people in ways that she'll never know."

All of the people at Pepe's keep a much closer eye on Fran since then. John the baker said, "It's everybody's worst fear—that we'll come in and find her dropped over dead." He paused solemnly for a moment and then added, "But knowing her, she probably still won't stop going for two or three days."

DIABETES

CHAPTER 17
Steve and Johnnie

It was a rainy April evening, the Tuesday before Easter. A limo driver stood in Chicago's O'Hare Airport holding a cardboard sign that read "Fran Tate." Feeling a tap on his shoulder, he turned around to see a 6-foot white rabbit with a basket over its arm standing behind him.

"Who are you looking for?" the rabbit asked.

"Fran Tate," he answered, reading his sign.

"That's me," said the rabbit. "Let's go."

They passed through the airport, the big rabbit giving small stuffed rabbits from the basket to the children that they met. The limousine drove the rabbit to the Hilton, where the desk clerk took his unusual guest in stride, merely remarking, "I've never checked in a bunny before. Would you like some carrots sent up to your room?"

The Easter Bunny's visit from Barrow to Chicago began years before when the hosts of an all-night Chicago radio show had an urge to talk to someone at the top of the world. Not knowing where to start, they called the police station in Barrow, and the police said, "Call Fran."

Their on-air phone conversations became a popular part of the show, and Fran obligingly answered questions about life in the far North. One night they asked what Barrow folks did for Easter.

"I told them, 'We're part of the United States, we do the same things you do. We have an Easter egg hunt—we hide the eggs in the snow,'" Fran said.

Barrow's Easter egg hunt usually occurs in conjunction with the spring festival, *Piuraagiaqta*. Spring above the Arctic Circle means sunlight, warmer temperatures and softening snow. The frozen lagoon in the middle of the town becomes the playing field for broom hockey, golf, tug-of-war, tea-making, maklak, and snow machine races. A battalion of front-end loaders and other heavy equipment clears the lagoon in preparation for the games, and the Easter egg hunt is held in the resulting hills of snow. The eggs are plastic, some of them containing gift certificates or other prizes. Experienced egg hunters arrive with big spoons and spatulas for digging in the snow.

"And," Fran told the callers, "I play the Easter Bunny every year."

She has been the Easter Bunny in Barrow since 1979, visiting the school and the hospital and riding the bus around town. Soon the radio personalities were wishing that the Easter Bunny could come to Chicago, and in no time Fran had bought herself a ticket and was flying east in a bunny suit.

Life After Dark, hosted by the husband and wife team Steve and Johnnie King, keeps night owls in more than 30 states company weeknights from 11 p.m. until 5 a.m. on WGN. After arriving in Chicago, Fran appeared on the show, then returned to her hotel for the briefest of naps. That morning, the Easter Bunny, accompanied by Steve and Johnnie, various hospital bigwigs, several reporters, and a fleet of news people from WGN-TV visited Children's Memorial Hospital, a five-story hospital for terminally ill children, many of whom are cancer patients.

"Don't mention Pepe's or Fran Tate," the Easter Bunny insisted. "Just say it's the Easter Bunny from WGN."

All day, the entourage crisscrossed the five floors of the hospital, arranging its visits around counseling and chemotherapy sessions. Every time the elevator doors opened on a new floor, the Easter Bunny swung into action, hopping and dancing and shaking her tail.

"Some of it was really pitiful," Fran said later. "I was glad I was inside that big head. Some of the children had no arms, no legs. The director of the hospital talked to me before we started to make sure I wouldn't say the wrong thing, like, 'How are you feeling?' They're probably feeling terrible.

"I remember one little girl about three years old. She had cancer and didn't have a bit of hair. She and her mama didn't speak any English. The Easter Bunny spoke a lot of Spanish that day. Her mother put a little hat on her head

Tacos on the Tundra

so she could have her picture taken with me. The hospital took Polaroid pictures of every kid with me and gave them the picture.

"One kid, who looked like he was ten or twelve years old, was black but he spoke Spanish. Both his arms were off at the shoulder. He was the hardest one for me to talk to. I just laid the Easter Bunny cup beside him. He was the saddest child. It was very difficult for me, but they said that I did well.

"It sure made me realize how neat little kids can be, kids who don't have any future at all. They have nothing to look forward to, except maybe tomorrow. One of the nurses said that by the time I left Chicago, four or five of those little kids would have died."

Eight hours after the big rabbit's arrival at the hospital, 580 terminally ill children had hugged and kissed the Easter Bunny, and 580 bunny cups had been given out from a huge wagon that the producer of Life After Dark pulled around the hospital.

"And not one kid reached in and took one," Fran said.

At 11 o'clock that night, the theme song for Life After Dark came on the air: "No more blue Chicago nights/ They're gonna make everything all right/ Steve and Johnnie, Johnnie and Steve."

After some opening remarks, Steve said, "Those of you who are long-time listeners know our relationship with Fran Tate, a lady from Barrow, Alaska, that we first had conversations with a few years ago."

Johnnie continued, "Fran has become a part of the show—she's become a character in our cast of characters."

Steve said, "A lot of listeners have sent cards to Fran, and she wanted to thank them, and she said that she would come down, literally for the day, and visit Children's Memorial Hospital. We did that today and it was an incredible experience. Fran, there's this wonderful transformation that happens when you put on a 25-pound head."

"Fran turns into the Easter Bunny," Johnnie said.

They recounted the day's highlights—the smiles and hugs, the child who hid under the bed, and the child who wanted to pull off the Easter Bunny's head.

Steve later wrote: "Kids who hated the idea of being in the hospital were suddenly transfixed (or maybe Fran-fixed) into laughing, happy kids, the way they're supposed to be."

Fran said, "There were a few kids, twelve or thirteen years old, who came up and hugged me and said, 'I love you, bunny,' just like they still believed in the Easter Bunny."

"After today," Steve said, "I still believe in the Easter Bunny."

Not one to dwell on past triumphs, Fran moved right into her favorite subject—Barrow.

"I noticed in the Chicago newspaper that eggs are 39 cents a dozen," she said. "At Pepe's North of the Border in Barrow, eggs are $1.57 a dozen, plus 18 cents a pound for freight. And that's wholesale!"

Tacos on the Tundra

"Stock up while you're here!" Johnnie urged her. "Put some in your suitcase."

Fran talked about her newly purchased freight truck and about the $3,000 it would cost to fly it up to Barrow. The old freight truck, originally purchased for the Elephant Pot Sewage Hauling business, had gone into retirement after the loss of its reverse gear.

"It's on its way to the dump," Fran said. "I just gave its fender a good-bye kiss the other day when I walked by."

The show was given over to listeners calling in to talk to Fran. The first caller asked if Mattie's Cafe was still in business and reminisced about the reindeer stew served there.

"Reindeer stew, that's pretty greasy stuff," Fran said. "And it's called Brower's Cafe these days."

Another caller who was planning to take a cruise to Alaska wanted to know what clothes to wear. Normally there are no cruise ships that come anywhere near the top of the world, but Fran jumped into her role of town booster and recommended Tundra Tours' one-day excursion. She warned that fog often extends one's visit. This led to a discussion of Barrow's weather.

"In the summer, believe it or not, people sit out in the sun on the beach all night, making bonfires and toasting hot dogs. It could be forty-five or fifty degrees, but we enjoy the sun as much as anybody. When it gets above seventy, it's hot, especially in the restaurant. We're all working in hot pants and tank tops!"

Another caller asked about "special privileges" for the Native population. Fran mentioned an ASRC dividend that was paid the previous spring.

"That dividend was $5,000 for each person that is a shareholder. The local snow machine dealer sold forty-one new snow machines that first day. So they have some privileges and rightly so. The land was theirs and still is. The oil companies came in and are making big money, so it's only fair."

Johnnie asked if people were saving their money.

"I don't think so," Fran answered. "It's a new culture for them, and they're caught between the old and the new. There are some people who are saving or upgrading their homes, but the general idea is to spend it. Fly to Anchorage and buy new clothes for the kids, or buy a pick-up truck—things that are important to them.

"When I first came to Barrow, jeans and straight hair—and not washed too often—were common. Now the Native girls get permanents, do their fingernails, wear pantyhose. It's a whole new society, and I'm glad to have been there to see it."

At 10 o'clock Friday morning, the Easter Bunny stepped off the plane in Barrow. She visited 21 kindergarten and first-grade classrooms, handed out more bunny cups and finally went home to collapse.

"Last time Steve and Johnnie called me, we talked about making this an annual event," Fran said. "That would be great! I'll probably be the Easter Bunny forever now."

CHAPTER 18
Community

Utpeagvik Presbyterian Church is a large white wooden structure with a bell tower. Its sign is carved on a whalebone scapula and supported by two whale ribs. Inside the church, the pews are rapidly filling. Most of the town is coming to the funeral of Magee, the Iñupiat woman who lived across the street from Pepe's. Her small house with dark green siding, built by her father from the remains of a shipwrecked schooner's cabin, had recently been improved by a large picture window. The window faced the street and allowed Magee, increasingly frail and less active, to keep an eye on the action on Agvik Street.

Magee paid for the window, but it was installed by Matt, Fran's all-around handyman, with Fran paying for the hours and finally days that he needed to cut through the solid cedar logs that made up her house.

Magee was a lively woman, more interested in others

than herself, a wonderful storyteller and hence, very popular. In the kitchen at Pepe's, along with the usual breakfast routine, the kitchen staff has kept an eye on a large ham that has spent the morning slowly baking. The ham will be delivered to the gathering of friends and family that will take place after the funeral.

"Any time there's a funeral, I donate a big cooked ham to the family on the evening of the funeral for their 'singspiration,' where they sing songs and give testimonials," Fran said. "I always deliver it myself, and when I come in the whole house is full, and everybody's hugging me.

"One January, starting New Year's Eve when a kid got shot, that month nine people died, and one of them was one of our favorite elders, Gilford Mongoyak. For his funeral, not only did I send a ham, but I made a big sheet cake that said 'God Bless You Gilford Mongoyak.' And someone at the restaurant was commenting on it, saying, 'Man, there's been a lot of funerals lately,' and I said, 'Yeah, nine hams and a cake!' And later on I thought, that's awfully cold. But that's how I related to it—nine hams and a cake.

"And then with the water company, we usually give them fifty or a hundred gallons of water the day of the funeral, because there's so many extra people in the house. We just chalk it up as a donation, and they know we do this, so sometimes they'll call and tell us when the funeral is, and Joe will go over and we don't charge them for it.

"One day a guy called and said, 'Do you deliver water to

dead people?' I said, 'Wait a minute. We don't deliver water to dead people.' He said, 'No, I mean when they die.' I said, 'What are you trying to tell me? I don't understand.' And he said, 'My uncle died in Anchorage, and I wondered if you'd bring me fifty gallons of water.'"

Fran has always respected and admired the elders of Barrow. Leslie Bagne, in charge of budget and grants compliance for the Barrow Health Department, remembered the opening of the town's first Senior Center. Bids were solicited from local providers for the hot lunch program. When the bids were opened, Fran's bid was considerably lower that the other four or five.

The Health Department knew her integrity and knew that she would be able to handle the job, but Bagne thought that the amount of money wouldn't be enough to cover Fran's costs.

Bagne said, "Fran was very insistent that she could provide quality food and felt that she owed something to the community. She's always loved and respected the elders, and she said that she wasn't going to make money on the Senior Center. Being a bit of a bureaucrat, I tried to convince her that there was nothing dishonest about making a certain wage for your work. But in the end, she got the contract, and, of course, she did a fabulous job.

"We had the same conversation every year, and Fran always got her way," Bagne said. "Fran always had the lowest bid, and continued to insist that she still made a profit and that she didn't need to make the bid any higher. She continued to provide food for the seniors until the new Senior Center, with its own kitchen, was built."

Any entertainment that Fran brought into Pepe's was always sent over to perform at the Senior Center.

Elise Patkotak remembered a mariachi group, brought up to Barrow for Pepe's fifth anniversary, that got the old women at the Center up dancing.

"The mariachis put their big sombreros on the old ladies' heads," Patkotak said. "Then the old ladies tried to get the old men up, but the old men would have nothing to do with it, and looked absolutely embarrassed by the whole thing. Only Fran would bring an entire mariachi band into the Senior Center and blow the roof off."

The customers in the restaurant thought the mariachis in full costume were hilarious. The band played every lunch and dinner and took requests from the audience. One woman asked them to play "Won Ton Tomato," which Fran eventually translated: "Guantanamera."

At first, it took some encouragement to bring the elders into Pepe's.

"That's how I started free dessert for Barrow senior citizens," Fran said. "At first, they didn't want to come in here—'That's too fancy,' they'd say. Or if they did come in, they'd never come any farther than the first tables.

"So I started giving them free pie and coffee. Now they want pie and coffee back in the dining room. Except Ida Numnik. She wants her blueberry pie right here in the coffee shop. But the Barrow seniors can have any kind of pie they want, and coffee, and ice cream. Free. I can name fifteen of them who are regulars.

"Then there's one fellow, he'll come in here and instead of pie, he'll want toast. I give him toast, call it 'pie' and don't charge him for it. Or a cup of soup. So he'll come in for breakfast, have toast and coffee, come in for lunch and have pie and ice cream, come in at supper and have a cup of soup, so I've supported him all day."

A sign advertising the free pie and ice cream hangs over the cash register.

"The sign now says 'Barrow Senior Citizens.' The sign first went up during the winter and just said 'Senior Citizens.' Then summer came and the first busload of tourists just about put me out of business. But now I've got a list of the seniors in town from the Senior Center, and I cross them off as they die."

On the Fourth of July, the Barrow community spends most of the day playing games. There are foot races for each age group, from two years old up to seventy years old and older. For several years, Fran would be at work in the restaurant when someone would call out that her age group was next. She'd go out, run the race, give the money that she won to 'the old people,' return to the restaurant and go back to work.

Pepe's always has a float in the town's Fourth of July parade. It's decorated in some patriotic fashion and constructed on whichever vehicle is available and running. Fran perches on it, wearing Stars and Stripes stockings and

COMMUNITY

an Uncle Sam top hat and throws out some inexpensive toys for the screaming kids that run along behind.

Fran sponsored a women's softball team, the Barrow Beauties, for twelve years, outfitting them in snazzy hot pink and black satin uniforms, carrying soft drinks down to the games, and treating them to free tacos when they won.

She began her Easter Bunny tradition in 1979 with a simpler brown rabbit suit. She rode the bus around the streets of Barrow, giving out hugs and candy.

"I remember the Easter Bunny hugging my two little girls, little girls who were in a strange, new place," said Leslie Bagne. "Fran was always wonderful with them."

In 1985, a magazine for American Jesuits ran an article about Barrow's Catholic church, which was built in 1954 from an abandoned military Quonset hut. The article described an Easter egg hunt on the ice, done with plastic eggs since real eggs would freeze. There is a picture of Fran as the Easter Bunny, "a 6-foot cotton-tailed Easter Bunny who stands in the midst of the children, handing out baskets and chocolate bunnies."

Barrow's fireworks are held on New Year's Eve rather than the Fourth of July, when the 24-hour daylight would take away most of the excitement. KBRW radio provides hot chocolate, commentary, and a special New Year's version of their program "Pagalatisi," Iñupiaq for "greetings to everyone." Listeners call in and extend New Year's wishes, some specific and personal and some extremely broad: "I'd

Tacos on the Tundra

like to wish everyone in Barrow and on the North Slope and in the whole world a Happy New Year!"

Every year Fran pays for most of the $4,000 worth of fireworks that light up the arctic night, as well as the airfares, hotel, and meals for the pyrotechnicians. And every year, Fran is down on the beach guarding the pile of fireworks covered with a tarp to protect them from a spark and keeping people—especially kids—away. She crouches under the tarp as fireworks are shot off some 20 feet away. Two men load the charges and two more act as runners, replenishing the supply from Fran's stockpile.

"I'm down there under the tarp with all the fireworks," Fran said. "You need the tarp because there's sparks flying around. I guess they figure if a spark lands on all those fireworks, the only thing they'll lose is one old lady. But you'll see me—I'll be in orbit."

Fran once calculated that she'd donated an average of $18,000 a year over a five-year period to local and worldwide causes.

"Every day I get requests. The other day they asked me to donate for prizes for the kids that are going to the college (Ilisagvik College, located in the old NARL complex) that had perfect attendance. I thought a diploma was what you won, not a Pepe's jacket or a T-shirt from Arctic Coast grocery store. Then the Presbyterian choir wants to go to Atqasuk. I've never even been to Atqasuk. I've been in this town twenty-five years and never been to one of the villages. If I go, I've got to pay my own way. Everybody else

COMMUNITY

gets Borough-funded trips all around."

She supports the Monterey Jazz Festival Scholarship, and Covenant House, a Catholic home for runaways. Once she bought a lot and donated the shack that stood on it to the volunteer firemen, who burned it down for practice.

But it was the little children in ballet classes at the Dance Theater of Harlem that really grabbed her interest.

"The Dance Theater of Harlem was on TV around 1985, on the program 60 Minutes," Fran said. "I never watch that because I'm always working then, but I must have been home at that time just to take care of the dogs."

Arthur Mitchell, the founder and director of the ballet school in Harlem, was being interviewed on the program. He mentioned that the school was having a difficult time financially. He gave the electric bill as an example, an expense that cost them $1,000 a month.

"I didn't have $1,000 extra," Fran said. "If you'd ask me for $1,000 today, I don't have it extra. But I'll borrow it from something else if I have to if it's for something I enjoy."

She sent the Dance Theater of Harlem a check for $1,000, saying, "here's for next month's light bill."

The company invited her to New York for their twentieth anniversary celebration, held at Lincoln Center.

"I was just in awe to see Lincoln Center," Fran said. "It's so big, they had the banquet in the lobby with an orchestra and everything. It cost you $500 just to sit in a chair, enjoy

197

the show and eat. I met Arthur Mitchell, the founder. I sat at the same table as the doctor for the company."

Other guests that evening were Bill Cosby, Dinah Merrill, and Donald Trump's brother, Robert, but it was Fran who was honored for being the person who came the farthest, probably in more ways than one.

"I was way out of my league," she said. "There were people wearing diamonds and emeralds. I was dressed appropriately, but my dress cost $89, while the one next to me probably cost five grand.

"I splurged on that trip and thought, that's a one-time thing, but then last year when I had my close call with death, I said, I'm going again.

"So I went to the twenty-fifth anniversary, and Bill Cosby was there again, and one of the ballerinas remembered me from five years ago. The company started out in the basement of a dirty old building and now they have a new school. I just donated money to buy ballet shoes for the school. I've probably donated way more than I can afford, but I just think they're so great."

In 1991, she saw the singers Hall and Oates being interviewed about a concert they were giving for the benefit of Alliance for the Appalachians. She boxed up 273 new Pepe's jackets, shirts and sweatpants. In the enclosed letter, she explained that "in business, you update the souvenir items every couple years." She added, "My main concern is that these clothing items actually reach the needy in Appalachia and not get re-routed elsewhere. I have heard of so many 'gifts' that never reach the intended, and I don't want to get caught up in that kind of operation."

Another bout of housecleaning in the souvenir department in 1995 sent an equal amount of clothing to Tuenic, Mississippi. Fran said, "I called the superintendent of schools in Jackson, asking for the poorest group of high school students in the state, and they led me to Tuenic.

"Pepe's gives so much to the local Eskimo community, I just wanted to do it elsewhere where the students might really enjoy a lift for the day."

After Hurricane Hugo devastated southern Florida, Fran heard that there was a desperate need for clothing, and another shipment of Pepe's souvenirs was sent to Homestead. She watched the news for a glimpse of one of her sweatshirts, but it wasn't until a tourist from Florida said that her sister—a hurricane survivor who lost her home—had gotten one that Fran knew they'd made it to their destination.

In the Utpeagvik Presbyterian Church, the long service is drawing to a close. Family members and close friends gather around the coffin for a final prayer. An enormous spray of white flowers nearly covers Magee's coffin. There is no card and no acknowledgment made of the giver. Probably no more than one or two people in the church know that they came from Fran.

Chapter 19
Jazz Below Zero

It's **4 minutes past noon** in the studio of KBRW, Barrow's only radio station. At noon, Elise Patkotak finished her 2-hour broadcast of Discount Radio, a loosely-formatted program of 60s rock 'n' roll, yard sale announcements, and off-beat news items. At exactly one minute after the hour, she patched into a satellite feed of National Public Radio news. Now she's nervously watching the red second hand swing around the big face of the studio clock.

"Come on, Fran," she mutters. She searches through a cabinet of compact discs. "Who is it that plays jazz? Miles Davis? Doesn't he play jazz?" She clutches the CD, mentally preparing herself for the challenge of hosting a jazz program. Her eyes return to the clock.

The studio door bangs open and Fran breezes in wearing a KBRW sweat suit and a black velvet bomber jacket with the word "JAZZ" sewn in silver thread on the back.

She glances at the studio clock.

"Oh man, it's my clock. My clock is off."

Elise eases out of the way, murmuring, "You've got thirty seconds." The black jacket and canvas bag of CDs hit the floor, and as the NPR news announcer signs off, Fran rolls the chair up to the mike, shoves the headset over her ears and smoothly announces, "This is Jazz Below Zero, KBRW, Barrow, Alaska."

She punches up the tape on which the latest weather update was recorded. The temperature is minus 20, minus 25 with the wind chill—a regular heat wave. When the nasal, corn-pone pronouncements of the National Weather Service announcer end, she adds, "If you just take a look at that full moon out there, you know it's going to be cold tonight, baby!"

She punches up another tape and the voice of jazz trumpet player Wynton Marsalis encourages everyone to "listen to my friend Fran Tate on the swingin' Jazz Below Zero—that's way below zero—on KBRW."

Fran first met Marsalis when he played in Anchorage. She went backstage to get his autograph and was told to wait by a door until he came out. After a long wait, she gave up and left the building. That's when she saw the long limousine parked outside.

"I thought, that guy ain't waiting for me, he's got to be waiting for Wynton and his group. So I went up to the driver and said, 'What would it cost for you to take me backstage?' and he said, 'Twenty bucks.' So I went back."

"I was the only white person there, not to mention the only blonde, so he noticed me right away, even if I am twice his age—three times his age. We had a nice conversation and I got his autograph on my program. Then next time he saw me, he remembered me."

The next time was three years later at the Monterey Jazz Festival. Fran stood in line to have him autograph his newest album. When it was finally her turn, he looked up and said, "Hi, Fran."

Always one to seize the moment, she immediately asked him for a interview to use on Jazz Below Zero. He said that he was booked up pretty tight, but told her to take a chance and wait in the cocktail lounge, where he would be conducting interviews later in the day.

When she got to the lounge, a crowd of reporters was already there, real reporters complete with name tags, cameras, notebooks, and "jackets with twenty-five different pockets."

"I thought, I'll never get there, all these VIPs will be ahead of me. But then Wynton came out, and there was some old guy who was paralyzed and in a wheelchair, just a jazz fan who wanted to say hi to him, so Wynton stopped and knelt down and talked to him. And talked to him. And talked to him. The media pack was surrounding him and I was over next to a trash can, but I was where I could see his eyes, so I just stood there by the trash can for about twenty minutes. Finally, Wynton stood up, and the reporters moved in, put the microphones in his face, saying, 'Wynton.' But he said, 'No, I've got an appointment with that lady right over there.'"

Fran's hand flutters over the KBRW logo on her chest. "Boy, my heart was going! I was one happy little turkey. After we finished the interview, he gave me a big hug and a kiss, and all I could say was, 'Wynton, if I was thirty years younger, nobody else would have a chance.' He is one very classy man."

The Dave Brubeck tune that began the program ends, and Fran reads off the Tundra Drum messages, an assortment of announcements that includes the usual meetings, rummage sales, and want ads of any community. But this is Bush Alaska and there are also a few personal messages. During whaling and hunting seasons, a large portion of the community is not accessible by phone, and there are messages like "Mom, we'll be back in Nuiqsut on the next plane that comes through, this coming from Nathaniel and John" and "Emma, my leg's not broke, I'll be home probably Tuesday." Today's announcements include one that ends with "This meeting has been canceled due to _____."

"I'm not reading this one," Fran says. "Screw that. Canceled due to what? They've got two weeks until the next meeting to figure out what they're doing." She tosses it aside and pulls the mike with a wind screen like a gray grapefruit closer to her.

Back on the air, she says, "You're listening to a program of new music, so new I haven't even heard it yet, I just now got these CDs in the mail. Now here's a tune by Richie Cole."

As the music begins, she tears at the cellophane packaging on the next CD with one hand and dials the number for the National Weather Service with the other. While "Tokyo Rose" plays, she records the latest weather update, neatly sliding it on the air just as the song ends.

"People think you just sit here and play music and don't do anything else," she says, laughing.

August 7, 1996, marked the sixteenth anniversary for Jazz Below Zero. The program began when someone at KBRW thought the station needed a jazz program and knew that Fran was a jazz fan. Much of the station's programming is done by volunteers with an interest in music.

"Somebody asked me if I wanted to volunteer and I said okay, but I never thought it would be anything that stuck. I didn't even know how to run a board. Someone else ran the board, cued up the records and I talked on the microphone. I didn't know how to do any of that, I was scared to death. It was an hour show, and we broadcast from the old station where Dorothy's Arctic Hair and Tanning Salon is now, with two turntables, and sometimes only one turntable worked. There were no tapes or CDs then. It was pretty rickety."

The show was later expanded to two hours. All the music on the show is from her own collection of 700 albums and 500 CDs. Fran's interest in jazz began in college.

"I learned that the drums are the basis of any music. They set the pace and the tempo continually. The jazz saxophone player can go off somewhere in left field and improvise all over the place, but it keeps coming back to the drum. That fascinated me. I listened to Miles Davis play 'My Funny Valentine,' and from there I started listening to more and collecting and reading about it."

In 1980, Western Airlines' in-flight magazine mentioned Fran in an article on jazz in the West.

"Anyone who feels unjustly deprived of jazz because his city doesn't have as much activity as Los Angeles or New York should reflect on how many Fran Tates there are in our midst, trying to spread the good word from a point where 55 degrees below zero is a nice, mild day."

Jazz Below Zero was recognized in 1990 as the longest-running radio broadcast in Alaska. Fran received the first Volunteer of the Year award from Alaska Public Radio Network.

She was at the Monterey Jazz Festival when the award was given, and the staff at KBRW conspired to have her call the station to hear the announcement during the pre-recorded Jazz Below Zero. KBRW operations director Mike McDermott said, "At first she couldn't believe it; then she broke down in tears with excitement."

"When I got off the phone, the people around me in Monterey thought I'd won the lottery," Fran said. "They were asking me, 'How much did you win?'"

In her thank you letter to APRN, Fran said, "When I

heard the news I was TOTALLY SURPRISED and ECSTATIC—WHEEEE! But it seems strange to get an award for volunteer work that you LOVE to do."

The song ends, and she's back on the air. "And this number features Christian McBride, my honey bunny coming up. He's one to watch, he's about twenty years old now, plays stand-up bass. Christian McBride, keep his name in mind."

She looks over a new blues CD.

"I've got to be careful playing blues. I've got one CD of a group called 'Uppity Blues Women.' It's three women, two black and one white, who all used to be schoolteachers. They're great, but they get so raunchy, there's only one cut on that whole CD that I can play. One song is called 'PMS Blues.' It's funny, but I wonder how they can get away with it.

"My mother made me play the violin—the 'wiolin,' she called it—because she always wanted to play the violin, but when she was a little girl, they didn't have any money, so she never got to play it, so she made me play it. And I hated the violin! Hated it! I wanted to play the saxophone, but she said 'that's a boy's instrument' and made me play the violin.

"Nine years I took violin lessons. Sometimes she couldn't pay for the lessons so she'd give the teacher a chicken or a dozen eggs. The night I graduated from high school, I smashed that violin up and threw it in the trash can.

"But I did learn how to play the bass fiddle and played in the swing band in high school. They built me a little stool to stand on because I was so short. I loved the bass fiddle.

"I finally bought an old beat up saxophone in a hock shop, and I've got to the point where I can just play 'Row, Row, Row Your Boat.' But the screeches are terrible."

Before opening Pepe's, she managed a jazz dance band called Below Zero, made up of "six blacks and a Puerto Rican." She soundproofed the garage at her Anchorage condo and made a studio so they could practice. They played the NCO clubs in military bases around the state, and well as private clubs, and were the opening band when artists like Kool and the Gang, James Brown, and the Staple Singers played Anchorage.

As manager of the band, Fran also functioned as hostess, getting the servicemen to dance.

"I'd allow only two dances with a guy, because pretty soon they get tighter to you than you really want to be. So I'd only allow two dances, but pretty soon everyone would be dancing."

She leans back into the microphone. "We're coming up to the final portion of Jazz Below Zero. We'll close out with my favorite musician, favorite player, favorite person, Wynton Marsalis."

Back in the kitchen at Pepe's, John the baker has the radio on. He says he likes listening to Fran on the radio: "It's the only time I can turn her off."

Chapter 20
Boss Lady

Fran asks a lot of her employees, but she treats them very well in return. In a glass case in the Fiesta Room, next to the piece of ivory with the delicate etching of the Pepe's logo, is a plaque proclaiming Fran "Boss of the Year 1969," a souvenir of the days when she ran the oil business.

"Anyone who helps me get to the top is on my side," she said. "I figure if I've got anything, they've helped me get it, so they deserve it too." She won many trips as prizes in oil sales promotional contests, trips to Bermuda, Las Vegas, Banff, and Puerta Vallarta. Each time, she gave them to the employees.

John Falk has worked at Pepe's off and on for eight years. His story is typical of many of her employees—a job opening for a cook, offering a salary plus room and board, listed at Job Service in Fairbanks. He got off the plane in Barrow at noon and was "on the line" dishing up tacos and enchiladas by 3 o'clock. Although he was originally hired as a breakfast cook, he was soon dividing his time between the Burger Barn and Pepe's, taking a short break in the afternoon, and putting in 12-hour days.

"She has a way of bringing out your talents, talents that you don't even know you have," he said. "Until I came up here, I had decorated one cake in my life, and that was my own wedding cake.

"But one day the baker decided to leave—got drunk, got on the plane, and that was all we saw of him. It was in 1988, when the whales were trapped in the ice. Every morning we'd start out making twelve dozen donuts for the guys out on the ice. Then the high school kids would pour in. The place was a zoo.

"Then Pancha asked me if I could decorate cakes. I'm an artist, I do paintings and sculptures, I figured a cake wasn't much different. After the baker left, it was like a crash course in cake decorating."

The first cake was for a Filipino child's first birthday, a major birthday celebration in the Filipino culture. The cake was a three-dimensional castle with towers built from sugar cubes, a drawbridge and flags. It took three and a half hours to decorate.

"We've done some interesting cakes—lots of 'boob cakes,'" he said. "Seems like every time there's a bachelor party, we do a half a dozen boob cakes. The most embarrassing cake I ever did was for a ladies' bachelorette party. Even Pancha got embarrassed."

Tacos on the Tundra

What did it look like?

"What do you think? Not only was it supposed to look realistic, it was supposed to look like it was working. So I took a little cornstarch and a little milk, made up a nice 'creme de menthe.' I got a $20 tip on that one. Girls were coming out to the kitchen, wanting to know who the model was."

The biggest cake he's made so far was for the National Bank of Alaska's tenth anniversary celebration, held in Barrow in 1991. Made to look like the bank's logo, it was really three huge sheet cakes put together and measured 3 feet by 6 feet.

"That reception was also the first time I had to do an ice sculpture. Pancha just walked up and said, 'Now, we need an ice sculpture. A whale. We've got plenty of ice, just go out and get a block and start carving.' She's a good example, she never says that she can't do something. As long as I've worked for her, she's never said, 'No, we can't handle that,' or 'No, we can't come up with that.' Right now, we've got a 45-pound pig in the oven for a Filipino party. It's so big we had to cut it in half to get it in the oven.

"The most challenging cakes to make are the wedding cakes 'to go.' I've done cakes—bake it, build it, take it apart, make drawings and instructions, put it in boxes and put them on the plane to fly out to one of the villages, and somebody out there puts it all back together. (In addition to Barrow, there are seven villages on the North Slope— Atqasuk, Point Lay, Point Hope, Kaktovik, Nuiqsut,

Anaktuvuk Pass, and Wainwright—with populations from 200 to 650. All of the villages, like Barrow itself, are accessible only by air. Unlike Barrow, which has jet service to Anchorage several times a day, the villages are serviced by small aircraft—the kind where you can sometimes sit up front with the pilot.)

"She tests your mental and physical capacity to the limit," John said. "There's always one more little thing that she wants you to do. I learned really fast that there's no way that you can physically keep up with her. The true challenge is reading her handwriting. She writes ninety miles an hour.

"She knows everything that's going on. She keeps track of everything. What's coming up this month, next month. She knows who's died, who's had a kid. She keeps it all in her head.

"She's a good boss," he said. "She knows when you need a hug and when you need a kick in the butt. When she's sees you're just to the limit, then she backs off.

"I guess it's one of those love-hate relationships, kind of like being married. Some days you look at her and you want to kill her, and other days she looks like this helpless nine-year-old that would be lost without you.

"But if you want to get her attention, you've got to call her 'Pancha.'"

Fran often takes Pepe's manager Bob Green on vacation as a bonus. They recently went to Vancouver, taking along the $3,300 in Canadian money that tourists spent at Pepe's and that Fran had been stuffing into a jar for years.

On March 27, 1990, when Fran picked up the Associated Press wire service stories from KBRW to do her daily "newspaper," she saw a story about a luxury train, the American European Express. A Chicago newspaper called the train the "chichi choochoo," and the *Saturday Evening Post* said it was "considered by many to be America's most luxurious travel experience."

The train, carrying a maximum of 166 passengers and a staff of 22, was made up of cars built in the 1940s and '50s by Union Pacific. A Florida developer bought them and spent more than $1 million each to refurbish them.

In the St. Moritz club car, with its black granite bar and embossed leather walls, a piano player played Gershwin and Cole Porter tunes on baby grand piano. The Milky Way was depicted in 23-karat gold leaf on the midnight blue ceiling. The baggage car also carried a health club, complete with sauna and masseuse. The observation car, built in 1948 for use on the Twentieth Century Limited, had a bar, parlor, and observation lounge.

After a champagne reception upon boarding, exquisite meals appeared about every two hours. In the dining cars, seven-course gourmet dinners were served on white linen and fine china, with breads freshly baked on the train. Dress on board ranged from formal evening wear to sophisticated business attire, with many of the men in black tie and the women in full-length gowns.

Although the train traveled from Chicago to several

eastern cities, Fran and Bob planned to ride the train's original route, from Chicago to Washington, D.C. The trip was to be a 12-year employee bonus for Bob.

Their reservations were made and changed several times for various reasons, and it wasn't until October 1993 that they were scheduled to go.

"The trip cost me $3,900, including the round-trip air fare," Fran said. "It was supposed to be a two-day trip, and they only selected so many people. The train had a baby grand piano and big candelabra in the lounge, and French cuisine—I couldn't even name the things they served. And it was only formal wear, full-length gowns. A lot of senators like to take that trip, they can live in the lap of luxury and they can get drunk and nobody else knows it.

"Bob and I left Barrow all decked out. We had only one set of kind of plain clothes for riding on the plane. After you're on the plane from Barrow to Chicago, you're ready for a shower.

"They said that when we got to Chicago, someone would be there with a limousine, carrying a sign that said 'American European Express.' I looked all over that airport and finally I got out the telephone number and called. They said, 'We've been trying to get hold of you all morning.' I said, 'All morning we've been on the plane coming from Anchorage to Chicago.' They told me that the company had filed Chapter Eleven bankruptcy that morning. I asked if they were going to give us accommodations in Chicago. They said they had no responsibility, and that we could file a claim with our travel agent.

"So here I've already spent $3,900 and we're stuck. I had about $1,000 cash with me, and Bob had his credit cards. We decided we'd stay and make it the best five days anyone could have in Chicago.

"We had to go shopping after we realized that the limousine was not going to pick us up. Bob had on a white suit, and I had on a long white dress, and we looked like a bride and groom going down the street. Bob said, 'Just take my arm and pretend that we just got married.'

"The first store we went into was a really expensive place, I. Magnin or Saks Fifth Avenue—some place like that. Bob's got champagne taste, so he picked out a sweater, a shirt, and a pair of corduroys. But I couldn't spend that much money, so I just wore my white dress until we found just a regular store.

"We stayed at the Chicago Hilton on the lake and did everything it was possible to do in that town. We went to blues and jazz clubs and ate something different three times a day because it's such a cosmopolitan town with all kinds of restaurants.

"We ate in a Peruvian restaurant that was five stars in the guidebook. It was a little tiny place, and they had all their awards hanging around. I ordered something, I had no idea what it was. Very spicy food. I always eat fish, so when I got my main dish, there was a piece of fish on one side of the plate. And the other side of the plate was kind of bare. I looked between the bare spot and something else they had there, and there was a little part of a Chore Girl—a sponge, like you use to wash pots.

"I didn't say anything. I'm not like some of our customers—'How gross! I'm not paying for this!' I ate around it, and I left it on the plate. There was a little piece of lettuce, so I put it on that, put my knife and fork across the plate. The waiter came, picked up the plate, very formal, and started walking toward the kitchen." Fran imitates the waiter doing a double take at the imaginary plate in her hand.

"About five minutes later he came back and apologized. I told him I was in the restaurant business, too, and I know those things can happen. But that was funny. Five stars.

"We went to the John Hancock Center and had dinner on the ninety-fifth floor. It cost us $395. We had a bottle of that champagne—Dom Perignon. I had swordfish for the first time, and the piece of swordfish wasn't very big. And there were three potatoes, about the size of marbles, and two little baby carrots on the side and a couple little strips of asparagus. If I'd really wanted to, I could have taken my fork, and hit them all. Bam, bam, bam!

"And the service. One maitre d' had only two tables, and he had four waiters working for him. I'd just barely drink a sip of water and I'd see a hand come in to fill it up. As soon as you'd mess up a little cube of butter, they'd replace it, they didn't want it to look bad. The maitre d' was standing there between the two tables, watching. I

Tacos on the Tundra

said, 'What is this—a Chevron station? Somebody's checking the oil, kicking the tires, washing the windshield—let me eat! Get your hands away from my food.' And Bob is from San Francisco where none of the buildings are very high because of the earthquakes, and we're on the ninety-fifth floor, overlooking Lake Michigan. He couldn't look out the window the whole time, it just scared him.

"But that was a trip and a half. I spent another $3,700 that week in Chicago. I spent another $600 or $700 on the attorney, but I never got any of my money back."

After 18 years, Bob retired with a generous allowance from Fran.

"A long time ago she told me, 'The longer you stay, the better off you'll be,'" he said.

"The hardest thing will be to leave Fran. We've done a lot of traveling together. She's been a true friend. She is the most outstanding, true-to-life person I've ever met. She's taught me a whole lot—my whole life has been here."

Boss Lady

Fran poses with Len Mink (alias Santa), a tourist from Baltimore.

CHAPTER 21
Tourists

The tourists from Tundra Tours have arrived. Like most of Barrow's visitors, they came in on the early plane, were picked up in reconditioned white school buses with "Tundra Tours" painted on the side in blue letters, were issued red and blue parkas to guard against the brisk 40-degree summer temperatures, and were taken on a tour of Barrow, ending with a cultural program by local Native dancers. Now they're hungry—rampantly hungry—and they all head for Pepe's.

They aren't the only ones. A private Christian tour group is also in town and they've reserved one of the dining rooms. Fran stands at the front entrance to make sure everyone ends up where they're supposed to be.

"Christian tour, this way," she repeats, pointing to the left. "Christians, over here. Sinners, that way." In contrast to the tourists who are shivering in their borrowed parkas, Fran is wearing shorts and a tank top.

Having 40 or 50 hungry people sit down at the same

time is not something a waiter or waitress likes to see, but it's part of the daily routine at Pepe's, and everyone springs into action. Fran whips back and forth across the dining room, seating people and distributing menus. One table of persistent customers grabs her attention as she flies by.

"Miss. Oh miss. We haven't given our order yet."

Fran puts on the brakes and gives them one of her looks.

"Where are you all from? South Dakota? Do they have cows in South Dakota?"

Yes, they have cows in South Dakota.

"When all those cows come into the barn at once, somebody's got to suck hind tit. Ain't no way you can milk all those cows at once. Now—somebody will be right with you."

On the tables are small printed cards that say, "While you are waiting, Pepe's thanks you!" Inside the card is written, "Thank you for selecting our establishment for your dining pleasure. Our personnel is trained to give prompt, courteous service along with our exciting Mexican-American dishes. BUT, we are in Barrow, and occasionally all systems register 'tilt': weather extremes; freight problems; unexpected crowds, especially at lunch hour; and other unique Barrow variables."

After everyone is seated, Fran gives a little speech. "We want to welcome all of you to Pepe's North of the Border and to Barrow. We'd like to have you sign our guestbook, which I'll bring around to your table, and we've got some souvenirs for you, a post card, an 'I Love Pepe's' button, and one of our very cheap pens. Sometimes they work, sometimes they don't."

A stuffed rabbit occupies a chair at one table. Its human companions explain that it's a stand-in for a friend who couldn't make the trip. Fran obligingly gives the souvenirs to the rabbit and poses for a picture with it.

One of the tourists is an enormous fellow, well over 6 feet tall and wide as a refrigerator. He is introduced to Fran as "Big Bill."

"I'd better introduce you to Big Bob," she says. "He's sitting right next door in the coffee shop." Fran exits to the coffee shop and returns with Big Bob Aiken, a Barrow man who describes himself as "the world's largest Eskimo."

Big Bill and Big Bob shake enormous hands, and it looks like Big Bill is a little bigger. There is a lot of good-natured banter, and cameras click as the two men pose together. Someone suggests that Fran pose between them, and another chorus of shutter-clicking begins. Someone has a Polaroid, and passes the developed photo to Fran, who whoops with laughter.

"I look like a skinny hot dog between two big buns!" she laughs. Turning to Big Bill she says, "You made my day. I'll buy you lunch."

A tour guide arrives with another group, hugs Fran and asks, "What have you been up to?"

"Clean livin' and hard work," she answers. "If you've got the hard work, you don't have time for anything else."

Most of the 8,000 yearly tourists and other visitors to Barrow find their way to Pepe's, and Fran greets nearly every one of them personally.

Tacos on the Tundra

"If you're in the people game, you've got to make everyone feel comfortable," she said.

But Fran doesn't put up with much nonsense, and sometimes diners get a piece of her mind along with their enchilada.

"The other day there was a woman here from New York, and she ordered a turkey sandwich. We use the deli smoked turkey, and they're nice, thick slices. Well, she said she didn't want that, she wanted fresh turkey. I said, 'You see a turkey farm out here?'"

One day a group of tourists arrived and stopped by the "Please wait to be seated" sign. Fran asked how many were in the party and one man answered, "Twenty-one." She asked him again and he said "twenty-one" again. Fran said, "Well, I can't seat twenty-one of you at the same table. You four sit over there."

Perhaps the man had been on the tour bus too long, but he started to shout that he was sick and tired of people telling him what to do and where to go and where to sit, and so on. Fran ignored him, and when everyone was finally seated, she introduced their waiter.

"This is Frederic, and he'll be your waiter." She moved off, throwing back over her shoulder, "and good luck!"

One evening a small group of tourists arrived. Fran went through her usual welcoming speech, passed around the guest book and handed out the souvenirs. She wandered over to look out the window while they turned their attention to the menu, until a man called over, "Is Pancha in tonight?" Without turning around, Fran said, "No, we gave her the night off," and then admitted that she and Pancha were one and the same.

Fran tries to be ready for everyone. She has ten menus printed in Braille. Although there are not many blind customers who make their way to Barrow, when one does come to Pepe's, their surprise and pleasure in having a menu that they can read is worth the $50 each that the menus cost.

Many visitors later write to Fran, often sending copies of the photos they've taken with her. One was a man from Virginia who visited Pepe's with his brother and their wives. Reacting to what seemed like high prices at the time, the man wrote in his letter, "Since your refried beans were $1.75 a serving, I suggested to my brother that I would get a dish and we would share them. You said, 'Don't be so cheap. Get two.' I said, 'Hell, woman—in Virginia I can get a whole pound of them for 39 cents.' You said, 'Well, buster, you get them 5,000 miles up here and see what they cost you.'"

The letter arrived with a pound bag of red beans, which the man admitted had cost him 67 cents a pound.

In the Fiesta Room, the tourists are already working on the souvenir postcards.

"Keep one and send the other," a woman says to her husband. "Did we send a card to the Hendersons?"

As the tourists attack their burritos and write their postcards, Fran works the room, asking "Where are you from?" and finding something to say about everyone's hometown, state, or country, sometimes in their own language.

"No more Wall," she says to a couple from East Germany. She and some people from Seattle have a short discussion about fishing. She talks about sumo wrestling with a Costa Rican woman. For a couple from Switzerland she sings a Swiss song and does a little yodel.

"My daddy yodeled and played the concertina," she tells them.

"I spoke four languages yesterday," she says. "Japanese, Spanish, German, and Texan!"

Someone in return asks her where she's from.

"I've lived here twenty-five years," she answers, laughing. "I've been here so long I can't remember where I'm from."

Fran gives a KBRW coffee mug to a tourist who was interested in the local radio station. The woman thanks Fran warmly for the unexpected gift.

"I have a few left over from the annual fund drive," Fran says. "You seemed so interested, I thought you might like one."

A few latecomers arrive. Fran whips the dirty dishes off the only vacant table, and before the customers can remove their generic red and blue parkas, she is assuring them that their waitress will be right with them.

"In the meantime, where are you folks from?"

Chapter 22
The One-Woman Chamber of Commerce

Fran's Chamber of Commerce activities began when she was still in Auburn, in what must have been one of the country's livelier Chambers.

"I was real—eccentric," she said. "There were about sixty people in the Chamber. And the same old codgers would sit in the same place every meeting, talk about the same old stuff. Then you'd get new members and they didn't know who these old guys were who never mingled.

"So I got an old Swiss cow bell from my daddy, and I rang the bell, and made those people wearing glasses sit on one side of the room, and those without glasses sit on the other side. And the next week it would be light-colored suits on one side and dark-colored suits on the other side. I had something every week to make them mingle. At first they didn't want to, they didn't want to move. But after three or four weeks they said it wasn't a bad idea because they met people that they didn't even know were there.

"We had a membership drive, a competition between Auburn and another town. Of course, Auburn won. I got a hundred and four new members in ninety days. Anyone that was a new member, I'd pick them up in a limo, courtesy of the Buick dealership, take them to lunch and sign them up with the Chamber. Everybody thought I was crazy. It was already starting back then."

Because Fran always seems to be at the center of whatever is going on in Barrow, she has evolved into a one-woman Chamber of Commerce. Any requests for information somehow make their way into Pepe's mail box. Partly as a way to deal with this she produced a brochure about Barrow that answers the most frequently asked questions. All first-time visitors to Pepe's get a brochure, a pen, and an "I Love Pepe's" button.

Keeping up with the correspondence is sometimes quite a job, and there is always a pile of letters to answer. To make the job easier, Fran photocopies the letter and writes her answers in the margins. She pulls one out of the pile and reads it.

"Here's one—'I'm very interested in applying for work on a fish boat or in a cannery.' I wrote back, 'Not in this town. Ocean is frozen nine months of the year. Try Southeast.'"

Another letter asks about "seasonal recreational activities." Fran writes, "Four seasons here: Winter, winter, winter and not too cold."

"One guy came in here last summer and said, 'Hi, my

The One-Woman Chamber of Commerce

name's So-and-So. Remember me? I'm the guy you sent information to.' Well, I have sent information to so many people..."

"Here's one in Las Vegas who wants to relocate up here, and he wants to know if we have food stamps. 'Do you have a welfare program that is nearby, to assist a single male who has no money?' I told him, 'If you don't have any money and are counting on food stamps, Alaska is not for you.'"

CHAPTER 23
The Polar Bear Club

August 2 is Barrow's first official sunset and signals the end of summer, but at 8 p.m. the sun is still high in the sky. In fact, the sun will really only "set" for 20 minutes, when it makes a quick dip below the horizon. To celebrate the event, the group of people straggling down to the stony beach by the Top of the World Hotel are planning a brief dip of their own.

The wind is blowing at a relatively calm 15 mph, and the surface of the Chukchi Sea—the part of the Arctic Ocean that lies west of Point Barrow—is lightly rippled. There is enough ice hanging close to shore to make the photos interesting; after all, without the ice, this could be a bunch of people jumping into the ocean in New Jersey.

Fran strides across the coarse sand in sealskin bedroom slippers. She has abandoned her water bills and tortilla invoices for a few minutes in order to officially witness the initiation of a half dozen potential members of the Polar

The Polar Bear Club

Bear Club.

The new members-to-be are reluctant to remove their clothes in the 40-degree summer weather. Everyone looks as if, given the chance, they could just as easily forget the whole thing. But they've paid their $10 and Fran is waiting.

The gravel beach is used more for boating and seal-hunting than for bathing, and discarded bits of metal make it dangerous for bare feet. Clothing is painfully stripped off, and white, trembling feet are shoved into rubber thongs and old sneakers. There is a last-minute arranging of towels and clothing on the gravel and then, with a sudden scream, everyone runs into the water.

The rule of Polar Bear Club membership is total submersion, head and all. The initial plunge is a real heart-stopper, and unlike most watery situations, one never really gets "used to" this one. There are whoops and screams as heads pop out of the water. Half of the group rush right back out, but the others prolong the experience a bit and swim out to a nearby chunk of ice. A cocker spaniel swims out after her master and nonchalantly joins him on the ice floe, delighted by all the humans paddling around in the water with her.

Finally, everyone is back on shore, frantically towelling off and dragging clothing back on over wet skin. Fran hands out large round patches in red and blue that show a polar bear wearing red bathing trunks. Members also get a personalized certificate that notes the date, air temperature, water temperature, and wind chill at the time of their plunge. At the end of the year, they'll receive Fran's annual newsletter with photos of some of the foolhardy/intrepid initiates.

"I don't know how I got into this Polar Bear Club thing—I guess I got roped into it," Fran said. "The Polar Bear Club's been around a long time. When I came up here in 1970, I joined the Polar Bear Club out at NARL. Back then, you had to jump in the ocean and eat *mikigaq,* too. (Mikigaq is an Iñupiaq specialty, a mixture of fermented whale meat, maktak, tongue, and blood. It's an acquired taste.)

"Later it became the responsibility of the City of Barrow. Then they dumped it on the Chamber of Commerce. Then the Chamber of Commerce broke up, and it fell on me, since I was the last known president of the Chamber of Commerce.

"But now I've got it organized. I still have them make out the check to the Chamber of Commerce, which doesn't even exist any more. I opened a special account for the Polar Bear Club, so I can buy the patches and the certificates. Right now I don't have enough in there to pay for a new order of patches, so I need about twenty more memberships to cover that. So it's very non-profit! And time-consuming! But I've kept it up—just because.

"I don't mind going down to the beach once a day, but three days last week I went down two or three times. Two people jump in, then someone else hears about it and—

The Polar Bear Club

'Hey, I want to jump in, too!' Then a couple hours later, a few more people show up. 'Hey, I want to go in, too!' Well, hey! I've got a job! I've got other things to do than run up and down to the beach. Then I call the weather bureau and get the temperatures and the wind chill and type up the certificates. There's more to it than just jumping in the ocean."

Next door to Pepe's, the Top of the World Hotel sells a "Toe Dipper" certificate that attests that the bearer "braved the frigid temperatures of the Arctic Ocean at the farthest point north on the North American Continent." That can be had for a few dollars, but if you want to be a Polar Bear Club member, the key is total immersion. Fran checks heads for dampness and sends one shivering Japanese girl back three times before she is baptised to Fran's satisfaction.

"I had two guys the other day who jumped in out at the Point. They walked away from the tour bus and jumped in, then they came back here and said, 'We jumped in.' And I told them, 'It don't count. A *lot* of people tell me they jumped in. You got to have an official witness.' They said, 'That means we got to do it again?' and they did, jumped in right out here, bare-ass naked. One guy just took off his pants, went in and came right back out. But the other guy walked out on an ice berg with his clothes on. He got up there and first he took off his shirt, then his hat. Then he had a T-shirt, so he took that off. Then he turned around, so you saw his rear end instead of his front end, took off his pants and did a back flip off that ice berg with just his shoes on. And the water's not that deep there, I don't know how he landed. Then he climbed back on the ice and put his clothes on.

"There were two other guys who skinny-dipped and took pictures of each other. They sent me some pictures, and where the guy's walking out of the water with his arms out, they took a black felt-tip pen and put an 'X' over the family jewels.

"Like I haven't seen it all before."

The Polar Bear Club

■ペペ　　　　　　　　　　　　　　　　　地図P.150
Restaurant Pepe's
　Barrow AK99723　☎(907)852-8200●月～土曜6時～22時、日曜9時～21時●無休　入口は質素だが、中に入ると「ここがバロー？」と思えるような優雅な雰囲気。メキシコ料理を得意とするだけあって、闘牛やソンブレロの壁画や、ドライフラワーをあしらえたテーブル周りは南国の気分が濃厚だ。1978年のオープンで、観光客には寒暖計などのプレゼントがある。タコス、ブリット、フリジョールなどのスナックや、スパニッシュオムレツ11.25㌦など、メキシコ気分でどうぞ。

CHAPTER 24
The Japanese Connection

> ■ぺぺ
> Restaurant Pepe's
> Barrow AK99723 ☎(907)852-8200●
> 6時〜22時、日曜9時〜21時●無休 入
> だが、中に入ると「ここがバロー？」と思
> な優雅な雰囲気。メキシコ料理を得意と
> あって、闘牛やソンブレロの壁画や、ド
> ワーをあしらえたテーブル周りは南国の
> 厚だ。1978年のオープンで、観光客には
> どのプレゼントがある。タコス、ブリッ
> ジョールなどのスナックや、スパニッ

On February 19, 1942, President Roosevelt signed Executive Order 9066 giving the secretary of war the authorization to establish military areas "from which any and all persons may be excluded as deemed necessary or desirable." The "military areas" came to include most of the West Coast, and the excluded people were the Japanese-Americans.

Between 1942 and 1946, more than 120,000 people of Japanese descent, 65 percent of whom were U.S. citizens, were imprisoned in what were euphemistically called "internment camps." When the Japanese residents of Auburn, Washington, Fran's hometown, were taken to internment camps, the town of 4,000 lost 20 percent of its population. Signs appeared in shop windows up and down Auburn's Main Street that said, "Banish the Japs from the coast forever."

It's easy to pick out Fran in her grade school class photographs. She's the one with the good legs, standing between her two best friends, Dorothy Terishima and Rose Shigeno.

"I grew up in a Japanese community," Fran said. "They didn't have any money, we didn't have any money. We traded chickens and goat milk with them for vegetables. You used to go down the roads where the Japanese farms were, and the rows were all perfect."

None of her friends were allowed to play after school; they all had to attend several hours of Japanese school to be educated in their language and culture. Fran was allowed to attend school with them, learning some of the language and the "courtesies."

The Natsuhara family, relatively well-off, owned a feed store. Fran had a crush on one of the sons, who was a few years older than her.

"I had a crush on Joe Natsuhara," Fran said. "He was my boyfriend, but he didn't know he was my boyfriend. I used to write his name on my notebook—'F.P. loves J.N.'—and I didn't want anybody to see it. But I did want somebody to see it. I probably never said ten words to him, but if I walked within ten feet of him, I got goose bumps. I remember he was missing part of a finger on his left hand from a farming accident. He was so smart. I had to work hard, but school work came right to him."

The Natsuharas, along with Fran's other Japanese friends, were sent to an internment camp in the spring of 1942. Natsuhara later remembered, "We were assembled

THE JAPANESE CONNECTION

along a railroad siding to be entrained. We were guarded by soldiers with rifles. As I looked along the tracks, I saw a small blonde girl saying goodbye to her friends. It was Fran, and she came to wish us well. I have not forgotten Fran's thoughtfulness, courage, and loyalty to her friends."

Nearly 50 years later, Fran looked up Joe Natsuhara. He wrote to her, saying, "I remember you very well because you came to bid us goodbye on the day we left Auburn for Pinedale Assembly Center in 1942. I remember you as a small little girl of thirteen at the railroad siding." Fran remembers crying bitterly as her friends were forced to leave their homes.

"The hardware store on the main street had a sign in the window about how much they hated the Japs," Fran said. "That's when I quit buying from them."

Natsuhara was sent to internment camps in Pinedale and Tule Lake, California, and Minidoka, Idaho. Along with the more than 30,000 children who attended school in the internment camps, he graduated from high school and—like many other Japanese-Americans—was drafted into the Army, in which he served for two years.

"And he went into the Army!" Fran said. "After they put him behind bars. Three of my high school classmates were in the United States Army and were killed fighting their own relatives."

Amy Iwasaki Mass, a social scientist who spent part of her childhood in an internment camp with her family, wrote in *Psychological Effects of the Camps:*

"Seeing the government as right and ourselves as somehow 'not O.K.' is the same psychological response that abused children use in viewing their relationships with their abusive parents...Japanese-Americans chose the cooperative, obedient American facade to cope with a overly hostile, racist America during World War II. By trying to prove we were 100 percent American, we hoped to be accepted."

In 1988, Congress passed the Civil Liberties Act, which included one-time, tax-free payments of $20,000 to surviving interns of the camps. Referring to the redress payments, Fran said, "No money will ever make up for that."

After the war, many returned to the Auburn area. They built a Buddhist church, where the Bon Odori festival is held each fall to celebrate the harvest.

"I know all the steps to the dance," Fran said. "I've got my own kimono, and I pin my hair up like they do, even if it is blonde. I would dance along with everyone else, and then spend the whole day eating and visiting. I was very well-accepted in the Japanese community."

Fran maintains that relationship, making a special effort to make the Japanese tourists who come to Pepe's feel welcome.

In the summer of 1991, two Japanese comedians and a crew from TV Ashani, one of the three major networks in Japan, arrived in Barrow. They were there to film a segment that would be part of a comedy special for New Year's Eve, a prime-time spot on Japanese television. The

The Japanese Connection

comedians, Tashiro Masashi and Kuwano Nobuyoshi, were as popular in Japan as Eddie Murphy or Steve Martin were in the United States.

Filming began with Barrow locals Charlie and Harry Brower, Jr. ferrying the whole operation out to the ice, 12 miles from shore. In the finished segment, the two comedians slog across the ice, presumably arriving from Japan. One slips and falls on—what else?—a banana peel. They see something in the distance, and we hear sultry "spy" music as the camera reveals Fran, in her bright-red flapper outfit, lounging on the ice in a director's chair. She welcomes them, saying, "Welcome, best-loved Japanese comedians. I love you," and blows them a kiss. Japanese subtitles translated her words for the viewers.

"I had to rehearse two or three times," Fran remembered. "In the restaurant, I can take orders from twenty-five people—steaks rare, medium-rare, salad dressing, drinks—and never write it down, never miss. But they gave me three lines to learn, and I'm not used to having someone telling me what to say. I've usually got my own lines."

She then asks the two for "passports, please" and sends them on their way. They arrive on the beach and are greeted by the Barrow Native Dance group who perform a welcome dance and a blanket toss. A little girl welcomes them to Barrow and tells them that a special limousine awaits them.

The "limousine" turns out to be a dog sled pulled by

four dogs from a local musher's team. The dogs were uncomfortable in the 40-degree heat, and the combined weight of the two rather hefty stars was too much for them to really pull across the sand. The musher tried to tell Kuwano to not really stand on the back of the sled, but something must have been lost in the translation, for when the director called for action—"Hai dozo!"—the dogs threw themselves forward, leaping into the air as if jerked by strings, but the sled didn't budge. Kuwano finally jumped off and the sled glided off over the sand.

The final scene was shot inside Pepe's, as the two comedians sat down to a meal of Native foods. Walrus, maktak, and bearded seal were served, attractively arranged Japanese-style by one of the crew members. The comedians themselves didn't know in advance what they would be eating, so their reactions, while overdone, had a genuine spontaneity. There was a bit of exaggerated silliness: Japanese tourists are always trying to order maktak, which was popular in Japan and produced by huge whaling ships, a practice that made Japan less than popular with American environmental groups.

This popular TV special increased Fran's fame among Japanese tourists. Pepe's is mentioned in at least three Japanese guidebooks about Alaska, and a large portion of Fran's Christmas card list—5,000 names long and growing every year—goes to Japan.

But it was only after her nearly fatal diabetic coma that Fran managed to make a trip to Japan, a trip that she had dreamed of her entire life.

She went with her longtime traveling companion Bob Green.

"He asked, 'Are you strong enough?' and I said, 'Let's just go. I don't know how long I'm going to live, and I want to see Japan before I die,'" Fran said. "I've been waiting all these years to make the trip." They spent 10 days there, doing everything that a tourist needs to do.

"I've made a list my whole life of things I wanted to do if I ever got to Japan," Fran said. "The Emperor's Palace, sumo wrestling, Kyoto, the Golden Pavilion, the Ginza, karaoke. We ate in little hole-in-the-wall restaurants in the Fishmarket. Bob and I were sitting at the sushi bar in one little place and he said, 'This is so exciting,' Then the soup was served to us in a little container, and he took off the lid and jumped back and said, 'I can't eat that, it's got fish eyes in it.' But I ate it."

"We went everywhere on buses and subways. We went to the Tokyo Dome, the big indoor baseball stadium. It's called 'The Big Egg' because that's what it's shaped like. Then they've got ice cream bars in the same shape.

"We only went on one organized tour, to the Emperor's Palace in Kyoto. It was an all-day tour and it was always, 'Okay, take your pictures, we've got to get on the bus.' I didn't come that far to spend fifteen minutes, I wanted to look around. We went back on our own to every place that we went on that tour.

"But the Japanese bathroom, the traditional ones, it's

like a urinal but on the ground, and it goes into a trough. So you've got to get way down. I went into the restroom in the park at the Emperor's Palace, and I looked in that thing on the floor, and there was a beetle, about seven inches long, solid black with big legs and big pincers on its head. I said, 'I ain't sticking my booty down there, not for anything!' I made Bob stand outside while I went in the men's side."

"But I just love Japan. If I ever retire, I think I'd like to live in Japan," Fran said. After a moment she quickly added, "Not that I can think about retiring!"

The Japanese Connection

Chapter 25
The Christmas Card Queen

It's mid-afternoon in mid-November, and a few Pepe's employees are taking advantage of a momentary lull. Ensconced in a booth in the coffee shop, they are working through names and addresses collected all year in the guest books in each of the dining rooms. Over the next few months they will hand-address and Fran will hand-sign more than 5,000 Christmas cards.

The Enormous Christmas Card List started about 1980, when the number of tourists coming to Barrow was still pretty insignificant, and the restaurant actually had slow times during the winter months. It began when Fran asked first-time visitors to sign the guest books that are kept in each dining room.

"I try to talk to everybody as they come in," Fran said. "How many restaurants do you go in to where someone comes over and asks, 'Where are you from?' or 'How you doing?' and makes you feel welcome? They're in a strange country, and they don't know these people up here at all. And the only thing I can do to make them get out of being uptight about just being a tourist is to talk to them and act crazy. I'm the brunt of all the jokes.

"Then they're happy to be here, and they realize they've been someplace. And we give them something for nothing. Even if they don't eat, I still have them sign the guest book and give them $3.11 worth of souvenirs, that's what they cost me. Per person, whether they eat or not. We have lots of them that just come through, sign the guest book, tell me they're from North Dakota, order one taco—cut it in half—and I lose money. But you don't lose money, you gain because when they go back to North Dakota, they say, 'We ate at Pepe's,' whether they ate a $20 meal or a $3 meal, and they say, 'Look at the things they gave us. If you go, be sure to go to Pepe's.' Their word-of-mouth advertises for what someone else will come and spend.

"They like those things that we give out, some of them have seen them all over the United States. Two people from Anchorage said that when they told their neighbors they were coming to Barrow, the neighbors told them to be sure and eat at Pepe's, and they named all the little souvenirs that we give out."

The first tourists came to Barrow in 1954, following the construction of the first hotel. There were between 200 and 300 that year. In the tourist season of 1995, there were nearly 9,000, with approximately 8,000 of them on an organized tour. Most of them made their way to Pepe's.

The Christmas Card Queen

Everyone who signs the book with a full name and address—"and we can read it"—gets a Christmas card or a calendar, whichever Fran decides to send out that year.

So they sign in, people from all over who are adrift at the top of the world and find some anchor of identity in a wacky woman's Mexican restaurant. They sign by the thousands, from the rich-and-famous to the regular folks. Pepe's and its famous guest book are mentioned in at least three Japanese guidebooks, and some Japanese tourists come back for a second or third time, clutching past season's Christmas cards in their hands.

What is especially amazing in this world of computers is that all of this is done by hand.

The work begins in the fall with staff spending their spare moments working their way through the guest books and beginning to address the envelopes. Fran insists that they keep them in order and insert a piece of paper for any that they can't decipher. Then Fran takes over, making another attempt to read the illegible ones, signing every card, and adding little personal notes to many of them.

"Sometimes when they sign the guest book, I put a little note beside their name, like 'very nice couple,' or 'doctor born thirty miles from my mom's hometown,' so when I come to them, I remember them, and I write something special. For a teacher, I might write, 'How's school?' For a birder, maybe 'Tweet tweet!'

"I can write 'Merry Christmas' in about ten different languages. I got it from something in the *Reader's Digest*.

They even have it in Armenian. There was a tourist here who was from Australia, but he was born in Armenia, and he signed the guest book in English and Armenian. So I wrote 'Merry Christmas' in Armenian and he wrote back and said that it's nice to know that he has an Armenian friend in Alaska. He should have figured out that I'm not Armenian."

Come December, Fran hauls them to the post office as they're finished, but some years the process takes a while. Sometimes the last ones go out in April; one year, it took until July.

"One smart aleck even sent me a Christmas card in May and said, 'Since you were late, I'm early, so here's Merry Christmas for next year.'"

Fran gets piles of mail in return, and everyone who writes gets added to the mailing list.

"They stay on until they don't answer no more," she said. "I've had some people on the list since 1981. I have several that I send birthday cards to. I answer all of it."

The shelves of her cramped, cluttered office are stacked with boxes. She opens one and pulls out handfuls of letters, postcards, and photographs of babies, weddings, and tourists posing in front of Pepe's. Some include Fran herself. A blue T-shirt decorated with signatures from a class of Florida second-graders thanks her for the Pepe's cups that she sent them. A small pair of reindeer skin boots sent by visiting Laplanders rests next to a pair of banderillas and a signed copy of George Meegan's book, *The Longest Walk*.

The Christmas Card Queen

A French tourist wrote that all he can remember about her are her legs, and enclosed a pair of lacy black stockings.

The Japanese tourists send silk scarves and tiny, exquisite origami; Australians tend to favor tea towels and calendars. She has a T-shirt from Germany that commemorates the collapse of the Berlin Wall, and a collection of baseball caps, T-shirts, and patches from nearly every state.

"One woman sent me a couple rings and a bracelet and said, 'I hope you don't mind my used jewelry.' No, that's fine, I'll take it," Fran said. "Bob says he thinks this one is a diamond. Beats me."

Another woman knitted Fran two hooded capes, enclosing a note that said she was "so worried about you up there in the Arctic."

The fan mail increased after her 1984 appearance on The Tonight Show and again in 1994, when both the Mark Russell special and Good Morning, America came to Alaska. With characteristic hyperbole, Russell said that "Pepe's North of the Border is the only thing that keeps Barrow from being a gulag."

What started out as something fun to do during the slow, dark months of early winter has grown into a massive—and expensive—undertaking.

"In 1993, the calendars cost 58 cents each just for the postage," Fran said. "And the Christmas cards to every foreign country except Mexico are 95 cents each for postage. About a third of the cards go to Japan. And then there's the cost of the items and the labor."

But it's not likely that the Christmas list will be cut back.

"I like Christmas. I don't like it for me—when I was a little girl, our Christmases were very poor, so Christmas was not a big thing. But after I grew up, I liked to give."

It's Christmas Eve, and the employees of Pepe's are having their Christmas party. A spangled tree stands at one end of the mirrored Fiesta Room, which has been decorated to a dizzying degree. Barrow-fashion, the gifts around the tree are swathed in black plastic trash bags.

Barrow is going through a "dry" cycle in which it is illegal to possess alcohol, so the party atmosphere is a bit strained. But the employees cheerfully remove their gifts from the plastic sacks—stylish personalized Pepe's jackets, tinned rum cakes as big as hub caps, and personal organizers in Italian leather. There are presents for Fran, too, most of which involve pigs, her favorite animal, in some way.

And how does Barrow's Christmas Card Queen spend Christmas Day?

"The days off—Thanksgiving, Christmas, and New Year's—I use as catch-up days because I can sit down here in the office and not answer the telephone," she said. "Last Christmas I did a whole month's worth of billing that I was behind on. I kept track of how many times the phone rang. Eighty-four times. We have been closed on Christmas Day for eighteen years. I even put an ad on TV every year saying, 'Merry Christmas from Pepe's, we're closed.'"

The Christmas Card Queen

CHAPTER 26
Work

"**The thing that saved me** most of my life was that I don't mind working," Fran said. "There's nothing that I won't do, paid or not paid. My very first job I said, 'Just let me work a week, and if you like me, you can hire me, and if not, you don't have to pay me.'

"I was a soda jerk at the Suzy Q, a soda fountain for shakes, sodas, swirls, ice cream. It had an old-fashioned type juke box system, where it was at your table. You'd flip through the pages, drop in a nickel, press the button, and someone would say, 'What number?' and you'd say, 'Twenty-four' and they'd play the record. They were in a central location, and it was piped into the restaurant.

"The old guy that owned it was about eighty years old. He was a real slim guy—wore a top hat, white shirt, bow tie, always dressed in black. He'd cook the special every day. At lunch time we'd have a crowd wanting the special.

Then they'd want drinks or some ice cream. We had banana splits, all kinds of concoctions. I could just barely reach the counter. It was all I could do to pull the handles on the levers. I was about thirteen.

"The whole time I was in school, I'd be up early to help milk the goats, go to school, do my paper route, work at the bowling alley, do my homework, go to bed about two o'clock and get up again at five."

"Even now, Joe will say, 'Just because you feel good, that doesn't mean I'm not tired.'

"'By the work, one knows the workman.' That's what was in my yearbook. And I was upset. Everyone else had 'The Most Likely to Succeed,' 'The Best-Looking,' 'The Peppiest.' But mine said, 'By the work, one knows the workman.' I thought, 'What the hell does that mean?' and figured I must be a real dud."

While she was a college student, Fran worked at the Swedish Hospital in Seattle.

"Bedpan commando. I put bedpans in places where I didn't even know you could *fit* one. I was on the surgical ward where people are in casts and have all kinds of tubes and pipes. There were a couple of ladies with face lifts. That was the first time I saw that. They had their faces strapped with big, wide bandages. I'd work all night at the hospital, and then I had an eight o'clock class, so there was just enough time for me to catch a bus and go to school.

"One summer I worked for Stokely-Van Camp in the cannery. I worked the night shift because you got fifteen cents more an hour than the day shift. I packed peas in institutional-size bags for freezing. They were all the same silly-ass peas, but we had to put labels on for all the different brands.

"I had this old green milk truck, open on both sides, that I called The Green Hornet. I took it to college with me, everybody thought I was crazy. We used to pile three or four of us across the front seat, with the person on the outside half on the running board, hanging on. One night I went around the corner and pitched one of my friends out into the ditch. I got around the corner and was driving down the road and somebody said, 'Mary's out.'"

Fran got a degree in engineering in 1950 from the University of Washington, finishing the program in just three years. There were only five other women in the entire engineering program at that time.

"It was really hard for me," Fran said. "I struggled a lot. There were a lot of guys who were getting back from World War II, and they'd had experience on radar and all. I probably worked ten times as many hours on my projects as they did on theirs. In mechanical drawing, my professor really helped me a lot. I don't know if I could have made it without that. I remember being as dumb as can be.

"I was the only girl in that mechanical drawing class. You would have to draw something—like that pile of books, say. And you'd have to draw it from the top side, bottom, all sides. Man, I studied hard. Some nights the girls would come up to the third floor of the dormitory and say, 'You better go to bed, you've been up here all night.' But I'd say, 'No, I've got just two more pages to do.'"

After a lifetime of work, people in Barrow speculate on when Fran is going to retire.

"When am I going to retire? When I get my bills paid! Nobody understands—I have all this stuff, but I have no money in the bank!

"The way I got into real estate was like this. BUECI (Barrow Utilities and Electric Co-op) pays a capital credit—the more water you buy, the more you get back. I've been in the water business so long, and I used to have three or four trucks going. I've bought thousands and thousands of dollars worth of water. BUECI uses your money for eleven years, then they pay you a percentage back. Now my checks are big because I bought so much water in the past.

"I could be stingy like a lot of these bastards are in this town, work in Barrow and sock it away and then leave and spend it all in the Lower 48. But I take the money and build something, stick my neck out, get my tail in a crack. I've done it with Barrow Utilities money, not Pepe's money because Pepe's ain't that profitable. But Iñupiat Water is profitable because I got cheap labor! If I had to pay a driver $20 an hour plus benefits, that would be a different story.

"When I got that first capital credit check from BUECI, I couldn't believe it. My mouth dropped so far, it practically got disengaged from my jaw. The guys from BUECI brought it over in person because they figured I would react crazy, and after it actually sank in, I just screamed 'til everyone in the coffee shop could hear me all the way in my office.

"But I like building things. I love construction. I love to wear my hard hat. I designed my own house in Auburn, with an oriental garden and fountains.

"Up here in Barrow, back in the good old days after I bought my first house, when somebody had a house they wanted to sell, they came to me. I bought old shacks and remodeled them."

Fran has a number of apartment buildings, all painted blue, in Barrow, and she has her choice of tenants. Since she keeps the apartments furnished and repaired, they are the most desirable rental housing in town.

"You could buy a lot or a house and a lot. But if the land was under the Bureau of Indian Affairs, it was called a 'restricted lot.' Then you had to get BIA and the owner to agree to make it 'unrestricted.' Or you could do what I did when I built the Burger Barn in 1985 and an apartment building that we call 'the corner pocket' because we had to build it on a lot that has a real sharp corner. I lease that land from BIA, and the money is divided among the heirs of the owner of the property. After fifteen years, the building will belong to the people who own the property. So in the year 2002, those owners will have a $400,000 building. By that time I should have made my money back on it, but I don't care because I don't do it for the money. I do it because I love construction. People in town call me a one-woman RELI program. (RELI stands for "Resident Employment and Living Improvement," a local program to improve housing and employ local workers.)

"I take old shacks and fix them up. I don't make money on all of them—sometimes I lose. The bank can tell you that."

Fran never gave up on the idea of a McDonald's franchise, and the Burger Barn may have been the next best thing. Six planeloads of freight brought the pre-fabricated building to Barrow. The building, looking like a cartoon red barn, was assembled on its pilings. Because it sat so high off the ground, a dirt ramp had to be built up to the drive-in window, and a little elevator contraption lowered the food.

"I will pay off the Burger Barn in 2002. I'll be seventy-two years old and will probably hobble up to the bank with a cane to pay off the last payment!" she said.

"But because I've got these properties, people think I'm rich. Owing all this money to everybody ain't 'rich!' I've got bills to pay! If I was rich, I wouldn't be in here at five o'clock every morning, cooking. I've been trying for days to find a cook! They last four hours, then say, 'I can't handle it.' I go home around three or four in the morning. I've put in eighteen- to twenty-hour days since 1978."

Work

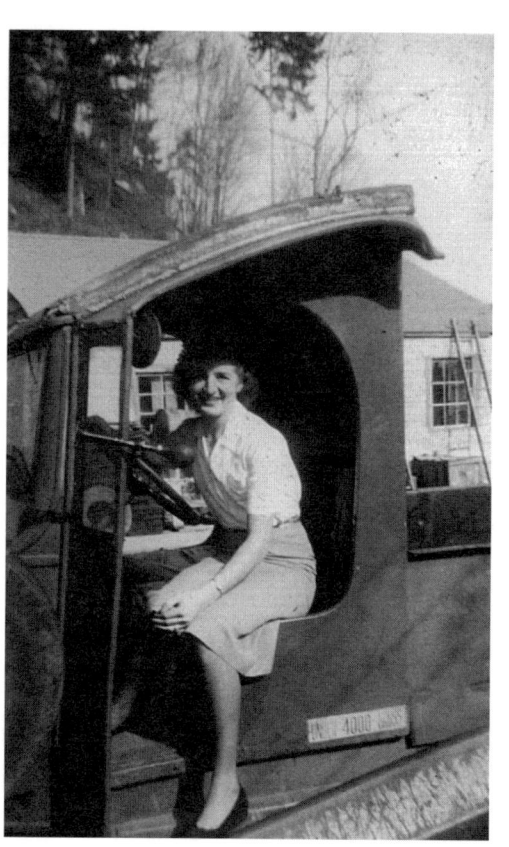

CHAPTER 27
The World According to Fran

F ran's oldest son Mike said, "For as long as I can remember, it's been 'Fran' and not 'Mom.' She called me 'Schults,' and I called her 'Fran.' She's been married a handful of times, but as far back as I can remember, she's been both my mom and my dad.

"If she's got a fault, it's that she's too honest. And she's always giving something away. When she ran the Fourth of July races, she would turn around and donate the prize money to 'the old folks,' and she wasn't all that young herself."

Leslie Bagne said, "She understands privacy and discretion. If you need to make unusual requests, she doesn't ask prying questions. One night a friend of ours was picked up and put in jail. The only way I could think to get cash for bail money in the middle of the night was Fran.

"I knew that she kept horrible work hours, and sure enough she was there at the restaurant, and when I asked her to cash a check and told her the amount, she said, 'No problem.' She never asked what it was for.

"I always found her to be extremely sensitive to different personalities," Bagne said. "I marvel at the amount of inner strength she has. She represents some things that people maybe wish they had a little more of—her courage, her willingness to try things. People live a little vicariously by that. She's been through hard times and never given up. We all need people who seem a little bit bigger that we are. Barrow people still recognize her as someone special."

George Meegan arrived in Barrow in 1990 after walking across North and South America from the tip of Tierra del Fuego, a trip that took him seven years.

"You always have to meet Fran when you come to Barrow" he said. "She's the legend. She's like Miss Kitty on 'Gunsmoke.' Maybe in a past life she was a Gold Rush madam who became mayor. She gave me dinner when I didn't have any money. She has a great heart."

Elise Patkotak summed up the feelings of many: "She's just such a presence, you can't imagine the world without her."

Fran became a grandmother when Mike and Cindy had two sons. After the second was born, Fran said, "Listen, I don't want to babysit. And don't call me 'Grandma.'"

They compromised by calling her *Akka*, the Iñupiaq word for grandmother.

"She could live with that," Mike said. "Now the kids call her 'Fran.' But back when she said, 'I don't want to babysit,' she also said, 'I want to make it right, so what do you need that will get me out of babysitting?'"

Mike said that there were two children but only one bed, and a week later there was a set of brand new bunk beds delivered with a note from Fran: "Don't EVER ask me to babysit. See you later."

Fran wasn't particularly interested in her grandsons as babies.

"I remember she held Alex like he was a sack of eggs," Mike said. "But when they got older and could work for her, that was a different story."

The oldest son went to Barrow when he was 12 years old and quickly found out that he couldn't keep up with his grandmother.

"He worked for about three days, and then he started making excuses and hiding out behind the Stuaqpak, just to get a break. He was supposed to be there a month, but after a week and a half, she sent him back," his father said.

"Then, when he was nineteen, he needed money for college. I was going to send him up to the Slope where I got him a job for $13.50 an hour, sixty hours a week, and Fran had a trailer she was going to let him live in. So this kid could have probably put $3,000 a month in his pocket, but in the end he didn't want to go. So our suspicions were confirmed—he was avoiding work at twelve and still avoiding it at nineteen."

"But Fran's a big dog lover," Mike said. "I'd like to die and come back as a dog in my mom's house."

"I always had dachshunds," Fran said. "My daddy was a dog lover, and we had two brown dachshunds, Cherie and Mitzi. My dad loved those doggies and he treated them just like humans. Cherie got so fat that the vet put a plastic cradle under her stomach with a wheel in the middle so her little belly wouldn't drag on the floor."

After Fran moved to Barrow, she got Hansel and Gretel as a Valentine's Day present from her son, Mike. Hansel was a long-haired and Gretel a short-haired dachshund. Gretel died recently at the ripe old age of 19; Hansel died three years before.

"He was my favorite dog," Fran said, "the most beautiful dog in the world."

When the Anchorage Concert Association sold bricks in Town Square, Fran placed a brick in Hansel's memory. Everytime she goes to Anchorage, she puts a flower on the brick that has the inscription, "In Loving Memory of My Dog, Hansie."

She also sent him to a Seattle taxidermist to be stuffed.

"They said they'd never done a dachshund before, but they would for me. I said I'd pay any price, but I've got to have my doggie." Hansie is in his old place, in Fran's living room. Periodic grooming keeps his long hair beautiful.

"When I die, I don't want to be buried like a normal Catholic. I want to give my body parts away. I hope my brain's still alright, I'll give that to the University of Alaska or some place.

"But I want to be cremated and I want Hansel and

Gretel to be cremated with me and we'll all be put in a little urn together. They've been my friends since forever. They've been with me when I'm happy, sad, hair's messed up, dinner's not ready—they don't care. My lawyer thinks it's crazy, but I don't care."

As the dogs got old, Fran cut the legs off her bed so they could still jump up. When she flew on Mark Air, she put the dogs on the seat next to her. Since Fran was such a good customer, the airline let her get away with it. Fran recently rescued two more dachshunds from the dog pound in Anchorage. At 5 and 9 years old, they were still very active.

"I think the two were mistreated. When I first got them, if I raised my arms to comb my hair, they would cower, like they were gonna get hit. The people that brought them to the pound said that they moved to an apartment where they couldn't have dogs. Now me—I'm a dog owner and I love my dogs. I'd find another apartment.

"I renamed those two—Fritz and Freida. Dachshunds, they've got to be German."

Fran once described herself in a letter as "a 'Plain Jane' who works hard, loves to work, loves people, loves goal-setting, and, more than that, accomplishing her goals." She also called herself the "crazy old blonde of the North."

"I am a crazy lady with a lot of guts. I believe that if you seek excellence, it takes guts; I have more guts than brains, so I do crazy things. Barrow is wonderful. I just love it, I can exercise all the crazy ideas I have right here.

Tacos on the Tundra

"As to a personal philosophy," Fran said, "if I had to do it all over, I would. I've had good and bad experiences.

"Nobody understands that there's trial and error and hardships as you move on your way up. Sure, you fall once in a while; I fall a lot of times. Everybody's afraid to fail. But you can't get to the top of the next mountain without going back down in the valley and starting all over again. I've gone down so many times, in businesses, in marriages, it don't make no difference.

"But it's fun working your way to the top. Once you're up there, if you're satisfied with that, that's cancerous complacency because you're comfortable there and you're afraid to go on to something or start something new, go down and start all over again. I've been at the bottom so many times, man, I don't care. It don't bother me.

"People can be so afraid to change. And some ideas are just hand-me-downs. I heard a story about someone's great-grandmother who just had a tiny little oven, and to cook a ham, she had to cut it in half. So when her daughter got married, every ham she'd cook she'd cut in half first. And so it went until 1967, when one of the great-granddaughters said, 'Why are you cutting the ham in half? The stove will hold the whole ham.' But everybody said, 'That's the way we've always done it.'"

"One of my favorite quotes is: 'God's gift to you is life; what you make out of your life is your gift to God.'"

TO ORDER EXTRA COPIES OF

TACOS ON THE TUNDRA

The story of Fran Tate, Barrow's most outrageous resident.

Please send me _____ **copies of**
Tacos on the Tundra @ $16.45/copy
(shipping included) . . . . $_____

WANT TO KNOW MORE ABOUT LIFE AT THE TOP OF THE WORLD?

BARROW, ALASKA
from A to Z

From A to Zero (and below)—everything you need to know about America's northern most community.

Please send me _____ **copies of**
Barrow, Alaska from A to Z @ $11.50/copy
(shipping included) . . . . $_____

TOTAL . . . . $_____

These books make wonderful gifts for anyone who loves Alaska.

Make checks payable to **Bonaparte Books**
Bonaparte Books
Box 139, 205 East Dimond Blvd.
Anchorage, Alaska 99515